MW00938260

Living His Dream

...and How He Helped Me Live Mine

Joey G. Cannady

WestBow
PRESS
A DIVISION OF THOMAS NELSON

WestBow Press books may be ordered through booksellers or by contacting:

WestBow Press
A Division of Thomas Nelson
1663 Liberty Drive
Bloomington, IN 47403
www.westbowpress.com
1-(866) 928-1240

Because of the dynamic nature of the Internet, any web addresses or links contained in this book may have changed since publication and may no longer be valid. The views expressed in this work are solely those of the author and do not necessarily reflect the views of the publisher, and the publisher hereby disclaims any responsibility for them.

Any people depicted in stock imagery provided by Thinkstock are models, and such images are being used for illustrative purposes only.

Certain stock imagery © Thinkstock.

ISBN: 978-1-4497-4572-1 (sc)
ISBN: 978-1-4497-4571-4 (e)
Library of Congress Control Number: 2012906682

Printed in the United States of America

WestBow Press rev. date: 4/17/2012

Special Thanks

I would like to give special thanks to my wife Karen, son Zac, and daughter Cassie Jo, for their love, inspiration, and support as I have ventured into this new endeavor of writing. I also offer special thanks to my sister, Teresa Lynn Cannady, for help with editing and formulating the words to share this great story of inspiration with you. May God bless each of them GREATLY!

Dedication

THIS BOOK IS DEDICATED TO everyone who has a dream in your heart that is yet unfilled. May you find the inspiration and courage to truly follow your heart, overcoming every obstacle, every difficulty, and every handicap that may be present in your life so that you may be able to proclaim, "I am Living My DREAM"

Our truest life is when we are in dreams awake.
Henry David Thoreau

When the best things are not possible, the best may be made of those that are.
Richard Hooker

Contents

Prologue

THE SAND MOUNTAIN REPORTER, OUR hometown newspaper, ran a large color photograph of my son, Zac Cannady, sitting tall and proud, headset atop his sandy blond hair, as he worked dispatch at the Albertville Police Department. Zac was wearing his blue golf shirt with a police badge on the front left chest and smiling, as he most often does, ear to ear. The caption read *Living His Dream*. It wasn't the first time Zac's dream had been a part of the local news. The Reporter published a story when he was seven years old in which Zac explained how he one day hoped to work for the police department; now he was doing just that and this amazing story had moved from dream to dream come true.

Police dispatcher — not a job that most of us would aspire to; but then most of us aren't anything like Zac. Zac is special, and not just because of the physical disabilities he faces every day, but because of his attitude, his love for others, his ability to inspire people around him. He'd dreamed of working for the police department for almost 15 years, carrying a police scanner almost everywhere he went, including the dinner table, much to our dismay, and memorizing every police scanner code number. Now he was getting up at 6 a.m. in the morning, no small task given Zac's physical disabilities, and working every day to serve the people of his city.

Zac was born with a congenital birth defect known as myleomeningocele, one of three forms of spina bifida (open spine) and also with Hydrocephalus (fluid on the brain). The spina bifida left him paralyzed below mid-chest and in a wheel chair for his entire life. The hydrocephalus required a shunt to drain spinal fluid from his brain and into his abdomen. Complicating his physical situation, he also suffers from extreme kyphosis (curved spine) causing him to lean forward, hampering lung function. Despite this myriad of physical complications, Zac rolls on – literally and figuratively. He was living with a shunt in his head, but a dream in his heart and now that dream has come true.

George Jones, the local reporter, interviewed Zac about his journey to what, at least for Zac, was the world's greatest job. As I read the newspaper article it was apparent that Zac not only knew what he had wanted, but went after it. At 22 years old he was able to proclaim what most of us can never say in a lifetime — "I am living my dream!" How did the dream start and where did this passion for law enforcement come from? How did Zac achieve what to many would be impossible? Well, that is what this book is all about! If you dare to dream and want to make that dream come true, come with me on this journey and learn as I have learned from Zac. He is an amazing teacher and a pretty amazing young man. Not only did Zac live his dream, but also he taught me how to live mine.

Here is his story, our story.

Joey G. Cannady, Zac's Dad

Chapter One

It Is Not How You Start but How You Finish

Living your dream is not just accomplishing a goal, getting the perfect job, or marrying that special person. Living your dream is a state of fulfillment. It gives you a sense that your life has a meaning; there is a specific purpose only you can fulfill. Living your dream is a state of mind, a satisfaction in your soul, and a realization that you, and what you do, matters! It is one of the most rewarding feelings you can have.

Achieving your life's dream requires a combination of several important ingredients. As I recently reread the news story about my son, Zac, God helped me to identify those ingredients and realize how they began developing from the day Zac was born. We all have the tendency to develop grandiose plans, to dream big about whom and what we can be in life, but too often, we give up on the trip before we even get the car out of the driveway. Since Zac's rocky beginning, I have realized the first of several principles to living your dream: it's not how you start, but how you finish that matters.

Zac's journey, as you will see it unfold in these pages, made me realize how little the start really matters, as long as you finish with what you wanted to achieve. The trip is an amazing, but often tricky, process. Zac had a very difficult beginning, one that almost ended before it even had a chance to begin. His journey has been inspiring, and his achievements have proved my point. Join me in that miraculous journey, with its ups and downs, smiles and frowns, to see how Zac was able to not only live his dream but also to show me—and allow me—to live mine!

Zachary Andrew Cannady was born on May 1, 1986, to Joey and Karen Cannady of Albertville, Alabama. Karen and I, like any young couple, looked forward to starting a family, raising our children, and enjoying the benefits of a small-town life. I worked as an accountant in Huntsville, a city one hour north of Albertville, and Karen worked as a receptionist in a local real-estate office. In the fall of 1985, Karen became pregnant with our first child, and excitement was in the air. We couldn't wait to welcome a little one into our home. There was much to do: pick colors and paint the nursery, put up the playful border, buy a new baby bed, and a host of other preparations necessary for a new baby.

However, in April of 1986, only one month from her due date and on a regular visit to the ob-gyn in Gadsden—a town thirty miles south of Albertville—our lives took a different turn. Karen, accompanied to this appointment by her mother, was informed there might be a problem and a sonogram was needed. The sonogram revealed that our baby boy had several serious, life threatening, and debilitating problems. The doctor diagnosed our child with spina bifida, commonly referred to as an open spine, as well as a condition known as hydrocephalus (fluid buildup on the brain). What a shock, out of the blue, and this late in the pregnancy. This would have been difficult enough for any mother, but especially so for a first time mother. Karen's mother phoned me at work to tell me there were complications with our baby and that I needed to meet them at the house as soon as possible. That was the longest trip home I'd ever made; in reality, it was only one hour, but it was an hour that seemed to pass in slow motion. I don't remember what was going through my mind, which is probably for the best, but I knew our lives would forever be changed no matter how the story finished.

At home, I was told the details of the complications our child faced. This was very difficult to hear. Shock, disbelief, frustration, anger, fear—all the emotions one could imagine swept over me like a crushing wave, and I felt unable to process what

I was hearing. Karen just wanted to be alone to think, or to not think at all, about what it all meant. The next few days were exhausting, filled with worry and wonder about what our future held.

Our doctor referred us to a specialist in Birmingham for more tests and confirmation of his diagnosis. A few days later, another sonogram at the University of Alabama–Birmingham (UAB) hospital not only confirmed the diagnosis but also brought even worse news. The doctor told us there was a high likelihood our baby didn't have any legs, and there were extreme deformities. Her advice was to deliver the child in the easiest way possible; she was convinced he couldn't survive outside the womb. We already felt as if we had been kicked in the gut, but now we got a second, and much harder, kick. We went home with our dreams dashed, our hope almost gone, facing a future filled with fear. We hibernated in the house. Karen did not want to face people and answer their questions about her pregnancy or the baby. Withdraw—that seemed like the best coping mechanism at that moment.

Slowly, time moved forward; days seemed like years. When would this nightmare end? The ob-gyn scheduled Karen for delivery on May 1, 1986, at Gadsden Baptist Hospital, with plans to induce labor. In the days before, I prayed fervently that God would allow everything to turn out okay, for the doctors to be wrong, and for our baby to be healthy. In the midst of this tumultuous time, I developed a peace I can describe only as a peace that passes understanding. However, that feeling of peace only masked a false hope that everything was going to be fine, or at least fine in the way I wanted it to be. I wanted the doctors to be wrong. I wanted our child to be perfect.

Early that morning, the doctor, through an intravenous medication, induced Karen's labor. She was a trooper, even as the pains intensified and the doctor recommended an epidural, a shot in the spine that blocks sensation below the waist. At first she refused, but eventually Karen agreed, and it was indeed a blessing to have this pain-reducing option. Around noon, it was clear the time for delivery was near, and Karen was taken to the delivery room. It was my first time to see the inside of a delivery room, complete with all the instruments and accessories necessary for bringing children into the world. Karen had a difficult labor, as the doctor tried to deliver our baby for more than an hour. There was pushing, pulling, the use of forceps; it was a trying ordeal, to say the least. Two nurses pushed on Karen's abdomen, while the doctor pulled on the baby's head with forceps—all to no avail, unfortunately. It seemed he wasn't ready to meet the world just yet. The whole process was an ugly and painful scene for me. Was this normal? I didn't know what was supposed to happen in a delivery room.

An hour later, the doctor finally decided that a cesarean section was the only option, and I watched in fear as Karen was prepped for this major surgical procedure. With everything in place, the doctor took the scalpel firmly and confidently in his hand and slid it from one side of Karen's abdomen to the other. Within minutes, the doctor reached his hands inside, and suddenly, out popped a head—a baby's head, our baby's head. Suddenly, the air changed. My head felt light, and I thought I was going to pass out! What a sight to behold, to see a baby—your very own son—being delivered from his mother's womb.

Fortunately, I collected myself, didn't pass out, and was able to experience the joy and miracle of our son, Zachary Andrew Cannady, being born at 1:36 p.m. But soon thereafter, the fears came rushing in: the fear he wouldn't live, the fear of what would happen next, the fear of his prognosis, assuming he survived. Then I heard him gasp his first breath, the nurse suctioned his mouth and nose, and there was Zac, alive and alert.

Within minutes, he was wrapped in a blanket and placed in my arms. I cannot begin to describe the flood of emotions that came over me. Here I was, holding my firstborn as he stared into my eyes, no doubt wondering who I was, where he was, and about all this excitement around him. As I carried him to the nursery, my heart and mind were racing, wondering, hoping for a better future than we had been led to believe. Most of all, I just wanted the medical professionals to take over and make him well. So I left him in the nursery as Karen was put to sleep for completion of the C-section. What an amazing, scary, long, and trying day this was turning into! But it was only getting started.

Within an hour, plans were made to transport Zac about fifty miles to the Children's Hospital of Alabama in Birmingham. Zac was placed in the nursery under the warming lights to await transport, and a nurse took some Polaroid pictures of him. Staring at those pictures, I realized how very rough he looked. I didn't appreciate how rough, since I had no frame of reference. This was my first experience with childbirth. Around three o'clock the transport team arrived, put Zac in a small plastic box with holes in the sides, and off he went, headed for Birmingham. Karen was now out of surgery and in recovery, waiting for a room. As soon as I determined she was stable, I jumped in the car with my parents and we raced to Birmingham, actually beating the ambulance to the hospital. Zac was immediately carried to a special care nursery. Only later would we realize just how special it truly was.

At Children's Hospital, Dr. Patricia Aronin, the head of Pediatric Neurology, examined Zac. I'll never forget her question, "What happened to this baby? He looks like he has been in a fight." I guess the pushing, pulling, and use of forceps for almost two hours had taken its toll on Zac. I wanted to respond: Yes, as a matter of fact, he has been in a fight—of sorts!

After the exam, Dr. Aronin led me to a small room and explained that Zac had Myleomenigocele, the most severe form of Spina Bifida, a congenital disorder caused by the incomplete closing of the embryonic neural tube. The opening on his spine was approximately two inches and you could actually see two vertebrate protruding through. She told me it was unlikely that he would never have any feeling in his lower extremities, and would have no bowel or bladder control. Dr. Aronin needed to close the opening as soon as possible, preventing germs from getting into the spinal fluid and creating other complications. She also explained that he had Hydrocephalus, causing spinal fluid to accumulate on his brain. He would need a shunt placed in his brain to drain the fluid.

It had been an extremely difficult day, but this discussion with Dr. Aronin was even more difficult. I sat, tears falling like rain, as she held my hand and offered encouragement. Afterwards, I went to the nursery to see Zac, lying in his tiny crib, now cleaned up and looking perfectly normal. Surgery was scheduled for the following morning, May 2nd, to close his spine.

We weren't allowed to spend the night in the nursery with Zac, so my parents and I left Birmingham around 7 p.m., returning to the Gadsden Baptist Hospital, to visit Karen and explain what Dr. Aronin had told me. Even though Karen was recovering from major surgery, she listened carefully, acknowledging ever word, and understanding as much as possible. Later that night we went home to attempt to sleep for a few hours, before returning to Children's Hospital at 8 a.m. We wanted to see Zac before he was taken to his first surgery.

Zachary Andrew Cannady—Day one, what a day! Who would imagine that the birth of your first-born son could present such a challenge? It was the first of many challenges to come but fortunately, there were many blessings to come as well. I had prayed fervently, begging God that Zac would be healthy, that everything would be ok, but at that moment things were far from ok. However, God's concept of ok and mine were not necessarily consistent. Now, looking back I can see that beginnings do not matter so much, certainly not by comparison with the finish. Zac had a hard start, a very hard start, but better days would come. It's not how you start, but how you finish that matters.

Has God placed a dream in your heart, one that you began, but haven't finished? Maybe you've had a difficult start, or a slow start, maybe you've given up along the way. What was exciting, fresh and new may have wilted under the weight of reality and the difficulties of life. Don't lose your dream, don't give up. I have learned from Zac, and in my own life, to focus on the finish; make your dream come true and achieve that ultimate goal. Press on, and don't lose hope; no challenge is too great, especially when it is life's greatest dream; your dream.

Chapter 2

Do Not Give Up Too Quickly

WHEN THE SUN CAME UP on May 2nd, there was renewed hope—hope for a better day, hope for a successful surgery, and hope for a better prognosis for Zac. My parents, sister, and I left home about 6 a.m. that Friday morning headed for Birmingham. With the morning light leading the way, we drove to Children's Hospital to visit Zac before he was rolled away to his first surgery, the first of many. In his hospital crib, he looked so tiny and helpless, but much improved compared to his first, very difficult day in this world.

At 8 a.m., Dr. Aronin and her team of pediatric neurologists took Zac for surgery. But before she joined them in the operating room, she explained the procedure in great detail, the entire family spellbound by her vivid description of the medical techniques. The procedure would entail incisions on each side of his torso from his armpits to his hips, pulling the skin over the open spine and sewing it together. Skin grafts from his buttocks and the back of his legs would be used to repair the incisions. For me, for all of us, it sounded like too much for a baby, not even twenty-four hours old, to endure. As I listened to this harrowing description of the surgery, my heart dropped into the pit of my stomach and another wave of grief rolled over my soul.

Given that the surgery would be more than four hours, Dr. Aronin suggested we find something to occupy our time. Following surgery Zac would be in recovery for at least another hour before returning to the Special Care Unit on the third floor of Children's Hospital, a place we would become all too familiar with in the coming months. Mom, Dad, my sister and I headed across the street to McDonalds for breakfast, not that we were hungry, but we needed a distraction. Even so, it was impossible to forget the circumstances and the danger Zac faced.

After ordering my food—a McDonald's Big Breakfast—I sat down in a booth near the window, the place filled with early more diners, though none of them seemed visible to me. I was in another world, and the next thing I can remember are the tears. Wave after wave of emotion came over me, my tears a waterfall into the scrambled eggs below me. There was no comfort, in food, in family, in anything that I could imagine. Zac was fighting for his life and as much as I wanted to help him in this struggle, there wasn't anything I could do at that moment. I was overtaken by the grief. The breakfast conversation was ominously sparse; none of us knew what to say, we just had to endure. We tried to eat but soon gave up and returned to the hospital. Even though there were hours of waiting ahead, we preferred to be close to Zac.

Those hours of waiting were barely tolerable, but we had no choice. As we sat, the clock ticking slowly, we wondered and worried about Karen, still in the Gadsden Baptist Hospital, and waited for news from Zac. Few words were spoken but many prayers were offered, mostly silent prayers, as we hoped against hope that all would be well, for Zac and Karen. Around noon, Dr. Aronin brought us news that the surgery had gone well; she had accomplished what she expected and was hopeful for good results. Zac would be returned to the Special Care Nursery within an hour if all went well, and fortunately it did, around 1 p.m. I was able to visit with him.

Four hours of surgery on a baby barely twenty-four hours old. Amazing! From Dr. Aronin's positive report I expected Zac to look—well, normal. But lacking experience with the effects of surgery, I was stunned when I saw him. It was unbelievable; Zac was wrapped in gauze, from beneath his arms to his thighs, he was one giant bandage. He was lying face down on his belly, stretched flat, and looking very scary.

Shortly after returning to the Special Care Nursery, Zac developed breathing problems, unable to maintain his oxygen level. As you can imagine, this created quite a disturbance in the unit, but the nurses responded quickly, placing him on oxygen, pumping vital air into his lungs. I was asked to leave while they stabilized him, but once outside, I peered thru a small window in the door to see what was happening with my baby. Once again, a wave of grief flooded over me, how much of this could he, or I, take. Fortunately, Dr. Aronin soon appeared to tell us the situation was under control and explain that children often have breathing difficult after surgery. Zac had lost a lot of blood, he was very weak, and given the circumstances this was a fairly normal response. I distinctly recall telling her, "Do not just keep him alive." I did not want him placed on a ventilator if he couldn't breathe on his own; there were already too many complications. I told her to just let him go.

Dr. Aronin's response revealed one of the key ingredients in living your dream. She told me, "Do not give up too quickly! He is going to make it, you must believe, just do not give up too quickly." She was right, we had to keep on believing, so we pulled ourselves together and prayed that the Lord's will be done—and just hung on for dear life, quite literally!

That day taught me that if you want to live your dream, you can't give up too quickly. When the going gets tough, we are often tempted to give in.

When hard times come, we want to find an easy way out, when what we should do is fight, and fight as if our life depended on it because sometimes it does. That day in Birmingham, I realized we had a fighter on our hands. Zac was not giving up and I certainly was not going to give up on him. Even though there was pain, grief, a struggle for life itself, there was no way I could give up on Zac. Zac's fighting spirit pulled him through the breathing struggles and many more struggles he would face in the future.

I stayed with him until about 6 p.m., sitting by his bedside, talking to him; the conversation pretty much one-sided. With so many family members wanting to visit, we divided our time, taking advantage of every minute we were allowed. We wanted Zac to know we were all there for him, pulling for him. In the months to come, my father would spend a great deal of time at Zac's bedside. Years later when Zac heard us talk about those visits, he would ask my dad, "Pop, what did we talk about when you visited me at the hospital?" Pop would just look at him and smile.

Thankfully Zac had made it through this first surgery and while it was a struggle, it was clear he was a fighter. We couldn't give up on him, no matter what happened. God had a plan; I could feel it, sense it, despite the pain and grief that sometimes caused us to momentarily lose our hope. We tried our best to remain positive and focus on that motto for the day—"Hang on, do not give up too quickly!"

In life, we are faced with situations that overwhelm us, knock us off our feet, even to our knees. When that happens to you, remember to hang on and do not give up too quickly. God has a plan for you to fulfill your dream, the dream he has placed within your heart. Sometimes that plan may seem lost in the darkness of life, but just hang on and do not give up too quickly. For in perseverance, you will be able to live your dream!

Chapter 3

Find the Silver Lining in Every Cloud

By Saturday May 3rd, our situation seemed to be improving. Karen was feeling much better and there was talk of her release from the hospital; finally a chance for her to see her new son. It was hard to imagine how difficult it was for her, having a new baby she couldn't see, hold, or express her love for. We were all suffering, trying to navigate this troubling time in our lives, but we worried about how difficult and painful it was for Zac. I took comfort in, hoped that, because of his paralysis, Zac couldn't feel a lot of the pain. For Karen, I was also thankful she had some time to rest in the hospital and not be faced with the reality we were living in Birmingham.

The weekend was approaching and we were hopeful that Karen would be released from the hospital on Monday. But for Zac, the situation took a turn for the worse on Sunday night. I was home alone, a very strange feeling, but after managing to get some things done around the house, I had fallen asleep. Around 1 a.m., I was awakened by the phone and well, as you might suspect, its never good news when a phone rings at that hour. A doctor from Children's Hospital, I didn't even get his name, was calling to tell me that Zac had been moved from the Special Care Unit to the Pediatric Intensive Care Unit (PICU). The PICU is for the most critical children, with one on one nursing care and a doctor in the unit at all times.

But the fact that Zac was moved to PICU was not even the bad news. The doctor asked, "Do you know what is wrong with your son?" Since Dr. Aronin had explained all the details about Spina Bifida and Zac's situation, I responded, "I think so." But apparently I didn't know as much as I thought. The doctor said that Zac had a broken right femur and a fractured skull. We needed to get to the hospital as soon as possible. The last few days had been crazy enough, now I was left wondering what in the world was going on; how could this even be happening? With no time to find the answers, I called my parents and within thirty minutes we were headed to Birmingham.

Sleepy headed and even more worried than before, I was still hopeful that things weren't as dire as the doctor described. I prepared myself for, what I thought was the worst, while trying to keep that hope for the best. Unfortunately, it was worse than I could have imagined. When I saw Zac at 3 a.m.

that morning, he appeared as before, lying on his stomach and wrapped in gauze, but now he was very swollen, like a balloon that had been over inflated. There were new complications we hadn't realized in the past two days. Zac had a broken leg and fractured skull as a result of the use of forceps and the excessive pushing and pulling during his attempted delivery. Dr. Aronin was right—he had been beaten up; not to mention that he had major surgery on his first day in this world. His body was tired, beaten and bruised, and he needed healing. But in that difficult moment I had a feeling, a gift from God, assuring me that everything would turn out well for Zac. It was a feeling that I found hard to believe, to hold on to with much hope, especially given the reality of his situation. So I asked the doctor, "What can you tell me that is positive; that is good for Zac?" I begged the doctor to tell me something, anything positive, about our situation. The doctor replied, "His heart is strong; his lungs are good and he seems to be a fighter." So there in the darkness of the night, and the darkness of life, there was hope, hope that Zac had enough fight to survive the challenges he faced.

You have to take what life gives you and make the best of it. In those dark hours I found a new way of looking at circumstances, one that I would later teach Zac—find the silver lining in every cloud. We have to believe, keep a positive attitude, and most of all not lose our hope. We can't let the reality of life, of a bad situation, stop us from believing that better days, better situations are indeed ahead.

Don't let your current reality overshadow the possibility of a better future. In that difficult time, I asked God to direct my thoughts to a positive place, to help me find that silver lining.

You too can find that silver lining, that hope to keep you on the path of your dreams. Find it, live with it, and even when the clouds seem to be closing in you will have the ability to make it through. On that fateful night, it was all I had, or at least all I could find in my heart, but it got me through and it got Zac through the night. Not only through the night, but also within forty-eight hours he was well enough to be transferred back to the Special Care Unit.

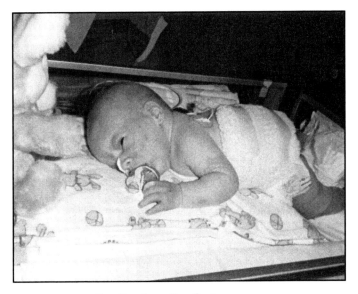

Zac the day after first surgery

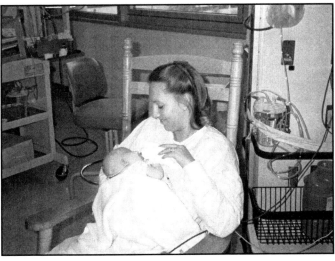

Karen holding Zac in Special Care Nursery

Chapter Four

Celebrate the Victories
Along the Way

As you work to accomplish a goal or live your dream, be sure to take some time to celebrate your victories. It will bring refreshment and add a little joy to difficult and stressful times, helping you to maintain a positive outlook on life and overcome the obstacles we all face. We learned this valuable lesson early in Zac's journey.

On Tuesday May 6th, Karen was released from the hospital and traveled to Birmingham to see her new baby boy. She was very excited to see him, despite what must have been much trepidation about how he would look, the condition he was in, the scariness of the hospital. Given the importance of the bonding process between mother and child, it was critical for Karen to spend time with Zac. The nurses were so kind and helpful arranging a way for her to hold him, despite all of the bandages. Zac was getting stronger each day, albeit slowly, and being able to spend several hours each day with him in the Special Care Nursery encouraged us. It was particularly helpful and encouraging for Karen and Zac, as well. She loved being able to hold him and talk to him, if only for several hours each day. I am not sure who was better from the experience, Karen or Zac, but either way it was a blessing for everyone to see Karen holding and loving Zac.

We were fast approaching that one-week milestone and the doctors and nurses began to prepare us for round two of surgery. This surgery would place a shunt in Zac's head to relieve the pressure of spinal fluid accumulating in his skull. On Friday morning, May 9th, Zac underwent surgery where a small opening was made, about the size of a dime, into his skull. A shunt was placed into the opening, connected to a long tube that ran from his head to his abdomen just underneath the skin, allowing fluid to drain from the inner part of his brain into his body. Pretty amazing technology! The surgery went well and Zac was back in the special care nursery in the afternoon, with only a small bandage, about a three inch square, on the back of his head. You could feel the shunt underneath the bandage. Fortunately, after this surgery, he looked much better than the previous week.

Even though the surgery went well, a new challenge arose when Zac began to have seizures. His eyes would roll back in his head, his body would stiffen, and begin shaking. The first time we witnessed a seizure it was very scary and extremely stressful for both Karen and me. I recall one particularly bad seizure that occurred while Karen was with him. The nurses sent her out of the unit while they worked with him. She left the nursery very upset and when we met in the hallway, we stood there, holding each other and crying. While the seizures were very scary for us to observe, the doctors and nurses knew what to do. Zac was put on Phenobarbital, a medicine to control seizures, which significantly reduced their occurrence.

Several days after the surgery, and once the seizures tapered off, Zac was moved to a special training room attached to the nursery where we stayed twenty four hours per day, as the nurses taught us to care for him at home. That was another entirely new experience, spending the night with Zac. We were taught how to handle him, move him, change him and dress him. The first night we did not sleep, trying to make sure everything was just right for Zac.

A week after the shunt surgery, on Friday May 16th, Zac was released from the hospital. What a day that was when we packed Zac and his supplies into our 1982 Honda Accord and headed toward Albertville. Given the dire predictions, the traumas Zac had faced, the two surgeries, and seizures, we were totally amazed and somewhat scared, to be going home. Not just home, but home with our son, Zac. Dr. Aronin told us to take him home, show him his nursery, enjoy him, and treat him as normal as possible!

What a thrill to pull into our driveway on Travis Street, and to see friends and family with *Welcome Home* signs, balloons and decorations, waiting patiently to meet Zac for the first time. It was truly a great day when we were able to celebrate his victory over surgery and illness, to celebrate the victory of finally being home, and most importantly, to celebrate his success in the struggle for life. Just a few weeks before, we couldn't have imagined seeing Zac at home in his crib. It was a great homecoming, and not just for Zac and us, but for our extended family and friends as well. It was great to be home, to put Zac in his room, and to hope for a better future. We truly enjoyed a celebration that day, filled with lots of hugs, kisses and even a few tears of joy.

That day taught me the importance of celebrating the victories. If you want to live your dream, you need to take time to celebrate the victories along the way, no matter how small or large. Even though they may seem small to you, they are successes— success that will build your confidence, get you past your struggles, and keep you in a positive frame of mind. Don't underestimate the power of the positive as a valuable tool in pursuing our dreams; be sure to celebrate the positive aspects daily. What do you have to celebrate? Find it, thank God for it and CELEBRATE every day those blessings from God—no matter how small or how large. Celebrating the victories will help fuel the fire to fulfill your dreams.

Chapter 5

Patience: Let Reality Catch Up With Your Dream

WHEN YOU ARE TRYING TO fulfill your dream, it can seem like tomorrow will never come; as if the outcome you hope for and long for may never arrive. As much as you may have hope, it can feel like reality doesn't match that dream. Have some patience; it takes time for the reality of your circumstances to catch up to your dream. This truth quickly became apparent in Zac's life.

What a thrill it was to be home. The past month and a half had truly been life altering for Karen and me and being at home with a new baby, especially a special needs baby, was yet another new, and frightening, experience. Karen moved Zac's bassinet into our bedroom, so he could sleep nearby. I will never forget waking up the first morning Zac was home. Karen, sleepy and anxious, looked at me with a definite fear in her eyes and said, "You go look!" Though neither of us wanted to say it out loud, both us were wondering if he had made it through the night. We were relieved and thrilled to find him doing just fine and ready for a bottle. Life was starting to be normal again—well, as normal as life can be with a new baby in the house.

Luckily, we had the support and prayers of people from every corner of Marshall County to help us return to normalcy; or at least to help us cope with our present reality. It wasn't until much later that I fully realized the extent of that support. Eight years later when I changed jobs, a new co-worker told me how he and his family had put Zac in their prayer journal when he was only a baby. In fact, their entire church, despite not knowing us personally, had prayed for Zac to be healthy and home where he belonged. What an amazing means of support, prayer—from people we had never met and how exciting to find, several years later, that we were connected to this family and this church through prayer.

Little did we know, in those early days, how much we needed those prayers. During our second week at home, I noticed Zac having difficultly taking his bottle; having never fed a baby, I didn't know what was normal, but something didn't seem right to me. Zac would become as listless as a rag doll when he was taking a bottle. In fact, I recall a picture of Karen's sister, Kathy, giving him a bottle while his arms hung limp beside his body. On our thirteenth day at home, while I was giving Zac his evening bottle, he collapsed and stopped breathing. Karen ran from the kitchen and began to scream as she saw him turning blue around his mouth and nose. I started CPR; Karen called 911, and then ran across the street to get help from our neighbor, Michele Reeves, who is a nurse. I continued CPR until Michele arrived and took over the process. Zac finally gasped and began to breathe on this own, just as the paramedics arrived; but he'd been without oxygen for at least seven minutes. The paramedics, realizing the seriousness of the situation, quickly transported him to the local hospital, and then on to Children's Hospital. Zac was transported by ambulance the sixty miles back to Children's and placed, once again, in the Special Care unit we had left only thirteen days before.

After examining Zac, the doctors found that he had difficulty breathing and swallowing at the same time. They weren't sure why this was happening, but knew that had to find a solution for him to receive nourishment. Their recommendation was to place a feeding tube in his stomach, a prospective that was horrifying to us. As if he didn't have enough problems, now we are told he may never be able to eat on his own. It was a tough decision to make, but our options were limited, basically to this one, at least at that point in time. We knew we had to do whatever it took, including the placement of the tube, to give Zac a chance for a decent future, at life itself. A feeding tube was placed in his stomach, along with a Nasogastric (NG) tube, which entered through his nose and sent formula directly to his stomach. The NG tube looked strange and uncomfortable, but as far as we could tell, it didn't seem to bother Zac. Most importantly, he could now get formula that would provide the nourishment he needed to survive, and move forward to meet the next challenge.

Despite those medical interventions, he continued to have difficulty with the formula. The doctor though it was reflux and resulting aspiration, causing the formula to flow into his lungs. To resolve this issue, the doctor recommended a surgery called fundoplication, whereby a section of his stomach was pulled around his esophagus preventing food from flowing upward. While the doctors felt it would solve the issue, the procedure was irreversible; again, another tough decision to be made. But we agreed to the surgery, which seemed to solve the problem.

Two weeks into the second hospital stay, Zac still had the feeding tube and the NG tube. We wanted to breathe easy and think we were done with surgery, but no such luck. A hernia was discovered in his abdomen and you guessed it, we were in for another surgery. To make a long story short, Zac underwent five surgeries during a six-week hospital stay. It was an extremely difficult time for all of us; but I couldn't imagine how difficult it must be for him.

After a few days of using the NG tube, the doctors wanted to give Zac some water, to test whether he might now be able to swallow. As you can imagine, we were very fearful of what might happen. That tiny bottle of water seemed like a gallon jug to us, and we were afraid he might choke to death. But fortunately, he responded well and with each day the amount of water was increased. Eventually they switched from water to formula, never having to use the feeding tube in his stomach. On the day the feeding tube was removed, we had a great sense of relief, knowing that one day he would be able to eat solid food.

Zac, now two months old, had only spent thirteen days outside of the hospital. But this situation was beyond our control and the experience taught me a new lesson–patience. Sometimes things do not happen the way you plan them; or even as doctors imagine they might. Just as we felt we had cleared the last hurdle, more trouble for Zac emerged. His shunt tube became blocked, requiring another surgery, known as shunt revision, to replace the valve in his skull. Fortunately, this procedure went very well and on July 5th he was well enough to return home. Even though we were happy to be headed home again, Karen and I were even more fearful than before. We knew how short lived it was before—a mere thirteen days—we hoped for better results this time.

Handling Zac's situation required a lot of patience on our part. We had to listen carefully and thoughtfully to the information the doctors gave us so that we could make the best decisions for his future, to ensure a healthy and productive life. But what choice did we have? One day as we exited Zac's hospital room, I overheard a doctor dictating his progress notes: "Even though his belly looks like a war zone, Zac Cannady is now a healthy baby." What refreshing words to finally hear, at last progress and hope that Zac was going to be well. The memory of those words stuck with me, not only because they were some of the most welcome since Zac's birth, but also because it was the 4th of July. From the hospital window we watched the fireworks explode in a myriad of colors over the city of Birmingham; commemorating not only the birth of a great nation, but my mother's forty-fifth birthday as well.

Sometimes we want to rush, to get things done quickly, in our own way and time, but our timetable is not always God's timetable. The reality of that taught me a new principal in life—for things to go according to plan, we must be patient. Remember, I felt that God had told me everything would turn out well, but so far the reality of life for Zac, and life with Zac, had certainly not caught up with that promise. If you want to live your dreams, there are going to be times when you must allow your hope for, and the promise of, that dream, to catch up with the reality of life. Yes, we want it all and we want it now; but God has His own timetable, which, more often than not, doesn't match ours. We need patience and lots of it. On July 5th, Zac was able to come home again, another milestone achieved. Thank the LORD! Patience had gotten us through and it can get you through as well, if you can hold on and let reality catch up with your dream.

Chapter 6

Use What You Have

With Zac free of the hospital, he could begin to live a more normal life. Even though there were regular visits to Children's hospital, at least he could now enjoy his own home, his own space. We very much enjoyed the "normal" life events like trips to the grocery store, football games on Friday night, and church on Sunday. We didn't feel quite comfortable leaving Zac alone in the church nursery, so either Karen or I would stay there with him. The upside was that he had an opportunity to be around other children, play with them, and make some friends. Life was good, as good as it had been in a long time, as good as it could be, for now.

Zac was growing and despite his paralysis, he developed his own brand of crawling. It looked a little strange to see him drag his lower body behind him, but he found his own way to move; a determination we would see repeated throughout his life. My mother always told us "can't never could do nothing," and can't was not for Zac, he just found his own way to can, whatever the challenge was. My mom helped with this challenge by making overalls for him that allowed him to crawl without pulling his pants off. His brand of crawling helped to build great upper body strength and with a bit of practice, he got good and fast, darting all over the house before we knew where he had gone. It was great fun to see him moving around, and he eventually got so strong that he could turn a forward flip; quite amazing for someone with such limited use of his lower body.

However, for him to have the mobility he needed to get out of the house he needed some special assistance. Children's Hospital came to the rescue with a small red wheelchair, made in Sweden. Zac loved his new "wheels" and was soon "running" around inside and out, enjoying this new found freedom. The wheelchair became a part of Zac's identity, his personality, and we came to expect seeing him in it. He loved getting outside, where we began to play baseball. He would sit at the plate, in that shiny red chair, waiting for each pitch I would throw with that small plastic baseball. With a little practice he could hit almost every pitch; he clearly had good eye-hand coordination, which continued to improve as he played other sports and grew to love video games.

With his wheelchair, Zac could get around easily at church and enjoy all the activities. Church has played a very large role in Zac's life, and ours as well. In 1987, when Zac was only one, we started attending Solitude Baptist Church in Albertville, Alabama. Zac quickly developed a love for music, especially for the old hymns. He had an amazing ability to memorize the lyrics to any song he heard and we spent many a joyous hour in his room listening to him sing. He couldn't seem to get enough of the music, it was a source of fun, and he seemed to have a real talent for it.

At age three, Zac attended Vacation Bible School for the first time; a week of fun filled with new experiences and new friends. On Sunday morning the children presented a commencement program, singing songs and repeating bible verses they learned during the last, very busy and eventful week. Zac, full of confidence and showmanship, informed his teacher that he wanted to sing during the program. So on that Sunday morning, in preparation for his first singing appearance, we dressed him in blue suit, white shirt and a red tie; he looked spectacular, a real little man. When the children lined up across the front of the church, most were a bit confused, as three year olds tend to be; but not Zac. He was handed a microphone and he started singing "Jesus Loves Me", solo. He knew every word and sang them with all the gusto he had inside, and that was a lot of gusto. It was a very moving experience, evoking a lot of feelings in the congregation that morning. People were crying, clearly touched by his amazing spirit and lack of fear to put himself out there. When the song was over Zac rolled back to his place like it was no big deal; to him it wasn't, just another day in Zac's life. On the way home from the commencement program, I asked Karen, "Did you see what just happened?" It was clear that Zac had a unique ability to touch people, an ability unlike one I'd ever seen before. It was a special day, a new experience in Zac's life, but only the first of many of occasions when Zac would take a microphone and sing his heart out.

Not surprisingly, singing became a big part of Zac's life. God had given Zac the talent, and the desire, to sing. He clearly didn't get the talent from me; that was his mother's gift—she is also a great singer, an alto with the voice of an angel. The two of them had a lot of good times learning songs together and even signing duets at church. At Antioch Baptist Church, where Karen's parents were members, her cousins played the piano and organ in what can only be called a very robust and energetic musical program. Zac's grandparents would bring audio tapes of their services, and even at a very young age, Zac would listen and sing along. An added benefit was that Zac was increasing his lung capacity. The ICU doctor said, when Zac was a newborn, he had good lungs and now he was able to use that ability to do something that would mean a lot, not only to himself, but also to the people around him. It was a blessing for Zac to build his skills as well as his faith, knowing that the words of those songs expressed the good gifts God has for us.

For Zac, it was more than talent, it was also a passion and passion is an integral part of living our dreams. God gives us abilities, people, opportunities in our lives—to bring love, enjoyment and to spark our passion. We've all been given talents; some more than others, but to each of us, God has given an ability that we are called upon to develop. Find, understand, and develop your potential, utilizing a passion that can make your dreams come true. Figure out what fuels that fire within you and as you ignite that fire, your life will take on a new meaning, a new purpose and you will see far reaching effects. Watching and learning from Zac, I realized we need to use what we have, no matter how big or small, for the Glory of God. Following your passion will move you in a positive direction, allowing you to live the dream God has placed in your heart.

How unfortunate that so many of us have never discovered that gift, that dream, or even if we have, we've been too fearful to follow it, develop it. Don't let fear foil your efforts, fear is not your friend; move forward with courage, knowing that if you take what you have and use it, you can make the dream come true. For Zac, delving into music was the beginning of a great adventure, which has brought joy and purpose, not only to his life, but also to countless others. How wonderful to live your dream, but how much better for it to bring hope and happiness to others around you. Don't miss out on your opportunity to do the same. Take what you have, add your own special brand of passion, and be a blessing to others. Don't get hung up on the depth or breadth of your talents, just use what you have and you'll see how far that can grow, what a difference it can make in the world. Use what you have—it's a critical ingredient in living your dream!

Chapter 7

Do Not Let Anyone Else Prevent You From Achieving What Only You Can Do

IN 1989, A WONDERFUL NEW blessing came to the Cannady household—a baby girl, one Zac quickly began to refer to as "my baby sister". On July 1, 1989, Cassie Jo Cannady was born, but not without an eventful entry into this world; it seemed a pattern was developing and not a good one. On May 19th, Karen, thirty-three weeks pregnant, was returning from her regular Ob-Gyn appointment in Gadsden; the same Ob-Gyn who delivered Zac. Zac was buckled in the child safety seat directly behind Karen in the 1987 Red Chevy Astro van we had purchased only a week before to accommodate Zac's wheelchair. As they were driving north on Highway 431 near Sardis, Alabama, another driver ran thru the median and struck the van on the left front and side, crashing the door in on Karen. Karen's stomach, more than seven months pregnant, almost touched the steering wheel as she drove, when the windshield broke, it cut her left arm badly. Although Zac remained locked in his safety seat the seat belt extended on impact, leaving him hanging off the edge of the car seat. Somehow, Karen managed to reach back and get Zac free and was holding him in her arms when I arrived.

At that time, I was working in Boaz, about five miles away when I received a call from a man who said, "Mr. Cannady, your wife has been in an accident, but I just want you to know she is doing fine." I responded, "Well how is our son?" The man replied, "All I can tell you is your wife is fine." What could that mean? I feared the worse, thinking something terrible had happened to Zac. I ran out of the office, jumped in my car, and was at the scene before the ambulance arrived.

And what a scene it was. The other car was in the middle of the highway with a woman lying beside it. Our van, along with Karen and Zac, was in the ditch. Blood was pouring from Karen's arm, but she was holding tight to Zac. When I reached her she simply said, "I'm fine!" I took Zac and within a few minutes the ambulance arrived, loaded Karen up and headed to the Gadsden Baptist Hospital. I put the car seat in my car, buckled Zac in, and followed the ambulance. Karen's arm was sewn up, she was fine in that respect; but the trauma of the wreck sent her into labor. Three years before, we were at this same hospital for the birth of Zac; now we were back again, with another trauma on our hands. Understandably, having seen his mother carried away in an ambulance, the chaos of the lights, the sirens, traumatized Zac. He was unnerved, and so was I for that matter.

The doctor determined that if "baby sister" was delivered she would only weigh about four pounds and her lungs wouldn't be sufficiently developed. Doctors began efforts to stop her labor but just in case they failed, we were asked to sign documents for labor and delivery. A transport team to take "baby sister" to Children's Hospital in Birmingham was also called. Was this all a bad dream? How could it be happening again? The doctor began an intravenous medication designed to stop the labor pains. While we prayed and hoped for the best, Karen remained in labor the rest of the afternoon and into the night. But finally, during the middle of the night the labor pains subsided. The medicine, or the prayers, or maybe a combination of both had worked. After a couple of days, Karen was sent home, with her stitched up arm, and placed on bed rest for the remaining seven weeks of the pregnancy. We hired a woman to stay with Karen and Zac in the daytime so she could rest and I was there to help at night. I was understandably worried about "baby sister," but the doctors assured us she was fine and in the safest place she could be until she was full term and ready to enter the world.

And what a spectacular entry "baby sister" made. Karen was scheduled for a caesarean section on July 3, 1989. However, on the morning of July 1st she awoke with labor pains; pains that went from every twenty minutes to every two minutes, in rather short order. Knowing the hospital was approximately forty minutes away, I called an ambulance, then called the family. My mother and sister came over to take care of Zac. Karen was loaded into the ambulance Around 6:30 a.m., but there was a problem. It was an Albertville City Ambulance, which couldn't transport her to Gadsden. An ambulance from the local hospital was quickly called but by the time they arrived the process was delayed another twenty minutes. By now I was frantic with fear that we wouldn't make it to the hospital in time.

Thankfully, the paramedics allowed me to ride in the back of the ambulance with her. We were speeding down Highway 431 headed south, passing the place where just seven weeks before Karen was involved in the wreck. Her labor pains were intense and it looked as if delivery was imminent, which was a scary situation since the doctor had advised us she needed a caesarean section. Because she'd had a caesarean with Zac, there was a danger of rupture at the incision. If that happened, she could bleed to death. Karen kept telling the paramedics they needed to check her; she felt the baby was about to come. With well-intended reassurance, the paramedic said, "Ma'am I have been doing this for twenty years and we've always made it to the hospital." Well, as they say, there is a first time for everything.

As we headed down the mountain, just inside the city limits of Attalla, Karen insisted that he check. When he lifted the blanket his eyes grew wide, I have never seen such stunned a look on anyone's face. The paramedic immediately told the driver to stop and pull over, saying, "We have to deliver now." He called ahead to the hospital and informed them that the baby was crowning and delivery was imminent. After two or three big pushes, it was done; easy for me to say, but extremely painful for Karen. Talk about natural childbirth — that's as natural as it gets. So at the foot of the mountain in Attalla on Highway 431 South, Karen gave birth to Cassie Jo Cannady, a seven pound, eight ounce "baby sister." They handed Cassie to Karen, wrapped in a sheet; what a beautiful sight to behold. The delivery complete, we got back on the road to the hospital, and my heart rate finally slowed down.

We were at the hospital within about ten minutes, where mother and baby were thoroughly examined and found to be doing well. Cassie was a beautiful healthy baby girl and the proudest person in the family was Zac; finally he had a "baby sister." My parents brought him to the hospital, where he proceeded to roll around the hospital in his little red wheel chair telling anyone who would listen that "he had a new baby sister, born in an ambulance." The funniest part was he could not pronounce sister correctly, but I think everyone got his point. Life held something new and exciting for him and for us, baby Cassie. Less than twenty four hours later, we were released from the hospital and we all headed home. Everyone was well and Zac really loved his new baby sister, life was truly good.

One of the greatest lessons I learned from these two children came about a year later. Zac and Cassie played together every day--—in the floor, in the baby bed, in the playpen. When she began to crawl, they would crawl together; it was very cute to see them racing across the floor together. One Saturday morning when Cassie was almost one, she and Zac were playing in her baby bed. I will never forget this moment. As they were playing Cassie pulled up, holding the rails of the baby bed, and stood up. Zac looked at her in amazement, turned to me and said, "Hey, she is standing up, baby sister is standing up." That was a very hard moment for me, seeing that he didn't understand why she could stand up and he could not. I remember trying to offer a reasonable explanation, an explanation a four year old could understand; but what I really wanted to do was run away and cry. Well, it seems my explanation was enough, as usual Zac took it all in stride, didn't make a big deal of it, and just moved on.

As I watched Zac grow and listened to him talk about his dream of becoming a police dispatcher, I began to understand this great truth. We can't let others define our limits. Often in life we give up on our dreams because we don't' believe we measure up to others. But not Zac, he wasn't going to allow what someone else could do, that he couldn't, to limit him. He was going to do what he was capable of, and that was going to be enough.

For the past ten years, I had felt a call from God to enter full-time ministry, but I failed to heed that call primarily because I never felt capable. I was sure someone else could a better job. I let that lack of belief in myself, my ability, my feeling of inadequacy keep me from what I was called to do. Not so for Zac; he would not let the fact that his sister could stand and eventually walk, keep him from achieving what only he could do. What an amazing revelation for me to learn from my 4-year-old—out of the mouths of babes.

If you want to live your dream, do not let the ability of others stop you from being all that God wants you to be—will help you to be, if you believe in yourself. Too often we refuse to do what we are capable of because we are convinced someone else is more capable. You have the power to do anything you choose, if you believe in yourself and follow God's plan. Live your DREAM! Zac has and eventually, thanks in part to his example, I would be able to also. Do not let anyone else prevent you from achieving what only you can.

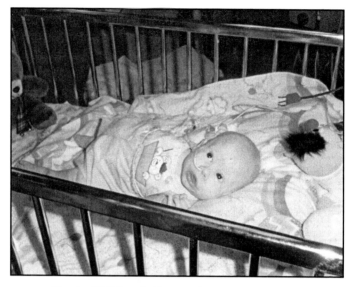

Zac in Children's Hospital with the Ng tube

Zac with Cassie standing in baby bed

Chapter 8

Adventure: Learn To Live a Little

LIVING OUR DREAMS MEANS NOT always playing it safe. Growing and learning, enjoying the dream, requires that we adventure into areas unknown to us. If we want to experience all that life has to offer and achieve our full potential, we need to try things we've never done before. We have to step out, or step up, take a chance and see what new gifts the opportunity can bring.

Zac has stepped out, figuratively, on a number of occasions and experienced thrilling moments in his life. His experiences have brought great learning to my life and there is one particular occasion that stands out. One Saturday morning when Zac was about five years old, we were planning to wash my 1982 Honda Accord, the one we brought Zac home from the hospital in. He was in his little red wheelchair, enjoying the freedom of rolling around the house, the yard, the neighborhood.

We gathered the washing supplies and headed out the front door. I turned my attention to filling the water bucket and when I looked up Zac was headed down our driveway and toward the street, a red streak in that little chair. I called for him to stop but he had something else in mind. His hands were on the armrest of the wheel chair, leaning slightly forward, he was moving faster than I'd ever seen the chair go. The driveway was about seventy feet long and sloped downward to the street in front of our house. Well, needless to say it was a fearful moment for me. I ran to try and catch up with him, but Zac was going too fast and had a good head start.

Thank God we lived on a dead end street with very little traffic because Zac zoomed right into the street. Fortunately, there was no traffic that morning when Zac flew across the street and into the ditch on the other side. When he hit the ditch the wheel chair flipped upside down leaving Zac face down in the wet and slightly muddy ditch. When I reached him, he was silent, so I quickly picked him up, asking "Zac are you hurt?" to which he replied, "No Dad I'm fine." Then I asked, "What are you doing racing down the driveway like that and flipping upside down in the ditch?" He simply replied, "I wanted to see what it felt like!"

What an amazing response. Zac simply wanted to see what it would feel like to get a full head of steam and roll as fast and as far as he could. He wanted to experience a little adventure of his own. I could easily understand that feeling, remembering my own childhood growing up in rural Alabama. As a young teenager, I had an Appaloosa horse, a mare, named Dixie. When we bought her, unbroken, and although I did not yet have a saddle, I was determined to go for a ride. I remember a television program where American Indians rode bareback in the old west and figured I could do the same. I had that same desire for adventure that Zac did, so I took Dixie an open field, grabbed two hands full of her manes and prompted her to run, as fast and as far as she wanted. What a feeling, as Dixie galloped faster and faster, the wind blowing thru my hair, as we crossed the field at full speed. I too, like Zac "just wanted to see how it would feel." We all need to experience some adventure in life; sometimes we just need to know how it feels.

Often in life we fail to reach our full potential or to live our dream because we are too cautious. We are afraid to take a chance and experience something new, something different, something truly exhilarating. There are times when we need to just let go and let the wind blow through our hair; to see what it feels like. Maybe you need a little adventure, to live a little, to see what it will feel like; on that Saturday morning Zac certainly did and you can too!

Chapter 9

Find the Faith to Make Your Dreams Come True

It is my personal belief that all true dreams for your life come from God. He is our Creator and God has placed a longing within each of our hearts. Zac began to develop serious longings at an early age; around age seven he was already interested in law enforcement and emergency Fire and Rescue. His interest began to develop when a police officer spoke at his elementary school. As the officer talked about his life, both the joys and pains of law enforcement, Zac made a connection. I am not sure if it was the thrill of the car chases or the idea of talking on the radio that piqued his interest, but nonethcless he was connected.

Before law enforcement grabbed his attention, Zac's was attracted to church, especially the music. We had taken Zac to church his entire life. Karen and

I attended Antioch Baptist church in Albertville even before Zac was born and both of us grew up attending church and believing in God. We certainly had a measure of faith, even though we were not as devoted as we should have been. When we learned of Zac's precarious situation, people all over Marshall County began to pray for us, and for Zac; I'm sure he was the most prayed for person I had ever seen.

Every night when I tucked him in to his red sports car waterbed, he and I would pray together. A waterbed is critical to avoid bedsores for people suffering from paralysis. Fortunately, we found a very fun and practical one for a child. It was a red race car with a spoiler as the headboard, a front end with headlights, and low to the floor so he could crawl in and out by himself. Each night before Zac went to sleep, I would lie beside his bed, we would lock thumbs, and say our nightly prayers.

On a Friday night in September 1993, when I tucked him into bed, I asked Zac if he was ready to pray. He responded strangely and said no, seemingly troubled. I told him that was fine, he didn't have to pray if he did not want to. I didn't want to force him to pray, so I left him alone and went to bed where I said my own prayers, praying for him as I had so many nights before. The next morning he was fine, we had a great day; nothing was mentioned about the previous night. However, that evening as we prepared for bed, I asked again if he was ready to say our prayers and he began to cry. I was very touched and upset that he seemed so bothered as to cry. When I asked what was wrong, he replied, "Dad if I die, I am going to hell." I was shocked and honestly did not know how to respond. I wondered what would make seven year old feel that way.

I did my best to explain, in terms a seven year old can understand, what I knew about salvation. I told him if he acknowledged he was a sinner, asked God's forgiveness and placed his faith and trust in Jesus Christ, in the death on the cross and the His resurrection from the dead, he would be saved. So Zac prayed very sincerely that night. Afterwards, I told him if he felt he had been saved, he should respond to the pastor's invitation after the sermon on Sunday morning, making a public acknowledgment of his faith.

The next morning after breakfast, we went to Solitude Baptist Church. Brother Jack Redfearn was our Pastor. When the invitation was given, Zac popped the brake loose on his wheel chair and headed to the front of the church. Zac shared with Brother Jack that he had asked God for forgiveness and accepted Jesus as his Savior last night in his bedroom. It was a wonderful day in the life of our church, everyone was very happy to see Zac make a profession of faith. Arrangements were made and a couple of weeks later, Brother Jack baptized Zac. What an amazing experience to see your son baptized. Not only see it, but to be a part of it; I actually got into the baptistery and held Zac up so Brother Jack could baptize him.

Faith is an important ingredient to living any dream. God's presence in our lives makes known to us the plans and the purposes for which we were created. God has certainly done that in Zac's life; he gave him the interest and passion for law enforcement, as well as the desire and talent to sing. If you want to live your dream, I encourage you to seek and know God. He is the source of all the dreams and many good gifts for your life. It takes real faith to understand and to make those dreams come true.

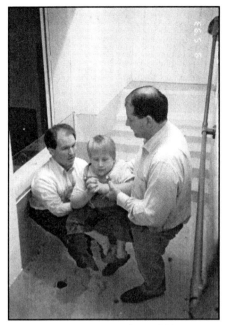

Zac - Baptized in 1993

Zac and "Best Bud" Shannon Sharit in her Auburn shirt

Chapter 10

Influence: The Impact on Other Lives

WHEN YOU LIVE A LIFE that allows your dreams to come true, you will find that events around you take on a new meaning and your influence is felt in ways you could never imagine. Zac, without deliberately meaning to, had a profound influence on a young woman who lived across the street from us. When Zac was only a few years old, Shannon Sharit, was our neighbor on Travis Street. During the years when Shannon was in middle school and high school, she would come over and play with Zac almost every day. She would roll him up and down the street in a wheelbarrow, like a load of dirt. It was quite a funny site to see Zac rolling past the house, sitting straight up in that wheelbarrow with Shannon at the handles. She would play games with him; his favorite was hitting a tennis ball with a small bat. They spent countless hours in the front yard or in his room, just having fun at whatever they did.

Zac found out that Shannon hated frogs and turtles. One day while Shannon was at school we saw a turtle crawling in the front yard. He decided to put it in our mailbox and then call Shannon after she got home from school and tell her that he left a gift for her in the mailbox. Late that afternoon Shannon walked over and opened the mailbox door, with Zac watching from his bedroom window. Naturally, Shannon almost jumped out of her skin and Zac laughed so hard he turned blue. Ever since that time, it has been an ongoing joke with them and they exchange gifts involving turtles and frogs, stuffed animals and similar items, always with a good laugh.

Shannon grew up with plans to be a schoolteacher and follow in her mother's footsteps, but a powerful influence led her in a different direction. When Zac was a small boy, Shannon would observe our neighbor and nurse, Michele Reeves, coming to our house to help. Shannon saw the help that Michelle could bring to Zac and wanted to experience that feeling herself. One day after we returned from an MRI at Children's Hospital, Shannon dropped by to find out how it went. She was concerned about the results and also knew that Zac had been afraid of the procedure. When Zac was telling her about the MRI, his focus was on the nurse who had been helpful to him that day. Zac talked on and on about the nurse and what she said, and how it allayed his concerned about the MRI. Shannon realized how wonderful it would be to help children in need, to help them overcome their fear, and have them remember her as fondly as Zac had remembered his nurse that day.

Still, when Shannon graduated from Albertville High School in 1990, she headed off to college planning to major in elementary education. But she soon had a change of heart, overtaken by the influence Zac had on her life. The plan to be a schoolteacher didn't seem so important anymore; she was being lead in another direction. She felt an overwhelming desire to become a nurse and work with children, and not just any children, but handicapped children. She changed her major and even changed universities, graduating with a degree in nursing from University of Alabama Birmingham and landing a job at Children's Hospital of Alabama. Shannon was assigned to work in the Special Care Unit, the same unit where Zac spent his early days. She was so influenced by Zac that she changed her life's plan and is now fulfilling her dream of nursing. Her entire career has been spent at Children's Hospital and she is now the Charge Nurse over the Special Care unit.

It is truly amazing the impact you can have on another person when you are living your dream. It is indeed possible to have influence in the determination of what others do and how they spend their lives. Zac and Shannon are great friends; they talk almost every day. Zac always knows how many children are in Shannon's unit at the hospital and what's going on in her life. One important thing they always discuss is the success of the Atlanta Braves baseball team; a favorite pastime they have shared for years. When Zac was only a few years old, they began discussing the Braves games and all these years later, they are still doing so.

There is one area in life that Zac has not been able to influence Shannon though. She is a very devout Auburn Tiger fan and Zac is an equally committed Alabama Crimson Tide fan. They have a lot of fun with this rivalry, teasing each other about their football teams. Zac has certainly not been able to influence Shannon to pull for the Tide, but he certainly has influenced her in other ways. Shannon also has influenced Zac; that is the beauty of their friendship. Zac has a wonderful picture of the two of them, Shannon in her Auburn shirt and Zac in his Alabama Shirt.

Influence is a powerful tool at our disposal; we all have an opportunity to impact the lives of others. Zac surely had had an important impact on Shannon. How amazing that she works in the very Hospital and special care unit where he got his start years before. At that desperate and scary time, we couldn't have imagined such an outcome for him or for Shannon. As you live your dreams, always be aware of your opportunity to influence others. Look for opportunities to reach out to others and help them live their dreams; you never know what may result. Remember Zac and Shannon, and know that you too, can have such an influence—influence that makes a difference!

Zac ready to sing at VBS

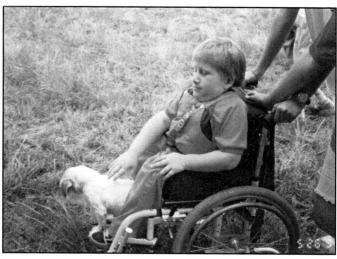

Zac with "Me Li" on his footrest

Chapter 11

Wear Your Passion!

In the spring of 1997, Zac, now eleven years old, was developing quiet an interest in sports. He loved his Alabama Crimson Tide football team; actually more than loved them, he'd developed a passion for it. Zac wanted to watch every game, know all the players and coaches names, and keep up with all the statistics. He could talk football with anyone; still can and does. Even now, Zac wears Alabama football shirts almost every day. The only exceptions are the occasional Atlanta Braves shirt or dress clothes for church.

On a Friday in late spring of 1997, we went to the Birmingham airport to pick up my sister, Teresa Cannady, who was arriving from China. We got to the airport early and were hanging around in the waiting area; this was pre-9/11 when you could actually go to the gates. Zac was dressed in all Alabama that day—cap, shirt, pants, and even shoes; he was completely decked out in crimson and white. Zac was rolling around the terminal, exploring curiously as he always did, when I noticed him talking to a man with a briefcase and wearing a trench coat. I thought I should check this out, so I made my way towards him. As I got close enough, I could hear them discussing Alabama football and the gentleman said, "So you are a real Alabama fan." Zac was telling him about the players he loved and in particular about Shaun Alexander. Shaun was a running back that season and they were sharing their mutual high hopes that he was going to have a big season. Zac talked like an expert sports commentator.

Just as I reached the two of them, I heard the man say to Zac, "My name is Andrew Sorensen and I am the President of the University of Alabama." He asked Zac if he would like to come to a football game in the fall, as his personal guest. Zac immediately looked up at me and asked, "Do you think we might can go dad?" I replied jokingly, "We will have to check our calendar, but I feel sure we could arrange something." Dr. Sorensen handed Zac his business card and told him to call his office on Monday morning and tell his assistant he was "the boy at the airport" and she would know what to do. As you can imagine Zac was thrilled, not only to meet Dr. Sorensen, but about the possibility of going to a game.

On Monday we called and just as Dr. Sorensen had promised his assistant knew what to do. She went through the schedule with us to pick a game. We decided that the game against the University of Houston on August 30, 1997, at Legion Field in Birmingham worked best for us because it was a daytime game and Birmingham was an hour and a half away. Dr. Sorensen's assistant asked if we could come early to meet "him and a few of his friends" for breakfast before the game. We were smart enough not to turn down such a special invitation; breakfast with the President of the University before the game, it doesn't get much better than that, at least not for an Alabama fan.

For months we talked about the game with great anticipation and when the day finally came, Karen, Zac and I, loaded up in our van and headed to Birmingham. We arrived around 9 a.m. and were escorted to the top floor of the hotel where we met Dr. Sorensen and a "few hundred" of his closest friends for a buffet breakfast. There were a lot of well-known people, dressed up, mingling and enjoying the morning meet and greet with the President. What an amazing opportunity for all of us; we were truly in for a treat, and it was just getting started.

After a great breakfast, we went downstairs and were loaded onto several luxury buses for the short ride to Legion Field. They placed Zac's wheelchair in the storage space under the bus and I carried Zac to a seat in the front. As we made our way along the streets of Birmingham, through blocked off intersections, with a police escort, it all seemed a bit surreal, like being in a movie. At the stadium the buses stopped at the press box entrance and we were escorted to an elevator and taken to the President's box. We were seated right next to Dr. Sorensen on the top row of the president's box at Legion Field. We were in awe! I had been to games at Legion field before, when I was younger, and remembered looking up at this very box and seeing the words along the bottom run of the upper deck, "Football Capital of the South." Now I was truly living a dream, sitting with Zac and Karen and the President of the University at opening day of the 1997 football season. How AWESOME is that? Zac loved it; he could see very well with no one walking in front of him. The front of the box was open, but an air conditioner was blowing behind us, so we stayed cool in the August Alabama heat. During the half-time performance of Alabama's "million dollar band," waiters in black suits and white gloves served a full meal of roast beef, mashed potatoes and gravy, and green beans.

On that fall day, at the first game of the season, we were all living a dream. Anything you wanted was brought to you, no need to leave your seat. All because Zac wore his Alabama gear, his passion, and wasn't afraid to talk to new people. His passion for what he so loved had led him to this great day. We watched Alabama win the home opener, the first game for the new head coach, Mike DuBose. Shaun Alexander played well and the final score was 42-17. There were 81,591 people in attendance at Legion Field that day, but no one had more fun than Zac Cannady, unless it was me!

What a wonderful gift we received, all thanks to Zac, wearing his passion at the airport. If you want to live your dream, really live it, you've got to wear your passion. Not just an Alabama shirt—or your team of choice—but whatever it is you are passionate about. Live that passion; do not just lumber aimlessly through another day. Live life with enthusiasm; with a desire to be the best you can, accomplish something positive in your life, and bring some light to the life of another person every day. That is wearing your passion—doing what you feel strongly about. I hope you get to live your dreams with gusto, like Zac did on Saturday, August 30, 1997. Wear your passion, wear it well, and it will help you live your dream.

Chapter 12

Friendship: You Can't Achieve Your Dreams Alone

We were never sure where Zac's love for law enforcement came from or what prompted his initial interest. At three years old, when the ambulance transported Karen from the car wreck to the hospital, he seemed very afraid of sirens. He would cry at sirens during parades. I assumed it had something to do with the shunt in his head; that perhaps it magnified the sound. But somewhere around seven years old he overcame his trepidation and suddenly began to love anything to do with Police and Fireman. I think it happened when Randy Amos, the Albertville Police Chief at that time, visited his school and gave a presentation about what policemen do. Randy and Zac quickly became friends and any time that Randy saw Zac, he would salute him.

Zac decided that he wanted a police scanner, so we bought him one and he began to listen to it almost non-stop. He learned all of the 10 codes—the police language for incidents; he would even talk to us in 10 codes. Zac would say there was a 10-50 at Highway 431 and Highway 75—that meant a wreck; or there was a 10-97 at Lazy Creek drive—that meant there was a fight occurring. Zac thought he had to know everything that happened in Marshall County, and thanks to his scanner, he pretty much did.

After mastering the 10 codes, Zac began to learn car numbers and radio call numbers for all of the local Policemen, and one particular Albertville police officer, officer number 130, stood out with Zac. His name was Richard Rutledge, a veteran of the force that everyone referred to simply as "Big R"—mostly because he was in fact a big man. I remember one particular day when we were at a local restaurant and Zac met Big R for the first time. Zac rolled across the room, right up to his table and said, "Hello 130, what about that call you went on this morning?" Big R loved it, and this was the beginning of a special friendship between the two of them; a friendship made in heaven, but based on a mutual passion in police work.

Big R was amazed that Zac knew so much about him—his call number, his car number, the calls he had been on that day. He developed a great love for Zac, stopping by our house to visit almost every week, sitting patiently with Zac, telling him police stories and updating him on everything going on around our small town. Zac truly loved these chats; they were the basis for his passion for law enforcement, giving him a good understanding for how the professional truly operates. Zac's relationship with Big R, led him to develop additional friendships with other officers on Big R's shift including Jeff Hall, Doug Pollard, and Jason Keeton, just to name a few. They all became part of Zac's circle of friends and helped him develop that love for law enforcement and his strong connection with the Albertville Police Department.

Big R graciously made arrangements for Zac to ride with him on patrol on Saturday mornings; an event Zac would wait anxiously for all week. He'd get up early on Saturday mornings, ready to hit the road, dressed in his police shirt and cap. Wherever Big R went on Saturday, Zac went with him. Big R was the captain of the shift, and as Zac described it, he was in the middle of all the "fun." But Zac seemed to be the one to have the real fun, especially when Big R allowed him to press that button that turns on the car sirens.

Zac developed a particular fondness for roadblocks where the police were conducting license and registration checks at selected locations. These roadblocks provided a lot of fun times, at least for Zac. For some unknown reason, he found it very funny when people got arrested or their car was towed away. One Saturday, Zac was with Big R while they were working a roadblock, checking drivers' license of everyone who passed through.

They detained a man because he had a hold on his license. The man couldn't seem to understand the explanation the young officer was giving him about how to resolve the problem, so he advised the man to speak to the Captain, Big R. The officer pointed to Big R's car where Zac was sitting in the front seat. Big R had stepped away from the car for a few minutes, so the man walked up to the car window and started discussing his situation with Zac. Zac listened attentively and then proceeded to tell him exactly what he needed to do, as if he was the man in charge. I guess in many ways Zac was the man in charge. As you can imagine, this is one of Zac's favorite stories and one we still laugh at every time he tells it.

Big R and Zac developed a special and lasting friendship that provided many happy memories for Zac. Big R attended Zac's birthday parties, school events, and even his High School graduation. At the graduation ceremony, Big R had the honor of presenting Zac with a tuition scholarship from the local police association in Marshall County. It was a very memorable day for both of them and the scholarship helped start Zac's formal education in Criminal Justice. In the fall Zac began his studies at Snead State Community College, where he later graduated with an Associate's degree in Criminal Justice. We have often laughed about whether the Criminal Justice degree was a "how to" or "how not to" degree. But since he worked for the police department and hasn't ended up in jail, at least so far, it must have been a how not to.

In 2004, Big R became very ill and was later diagnosed with cancer. To manage his health issues, he stopped working patrol and began office duty. Zac went to the police department every week and visited with Big R until he became unable to work and finally retired. You can be assured that Zac was at his side during the retirement party; Zac loved Big R and Big R loved Zac. This unique friendship played a major role in Zac's life and the development of his love for law enforcement; not to mention, how much it helped his practical education on how law enforcement really works.

Zac remained friends with Big R as he battled cancer, visiting him in the hospital and always bringing a smile. It was amazing and inspiring to see the love that developed between these two very unlikely people—this big police officer and this young man in a wheelchair. In 2006, Big R passed away. It was a very sad day at our house; we felt as if we had lost a member of our own family. Big R was quite possibly the closest friend Zac had ever had. Big R had requested that Zac serve as an honorary pallbearer at his funeral, which Zac was honored to do. The funeral home was crowded with policemen, family, and friends of this man who had devoted his life to serving others. A few days before he died, Big R wrote a letter, gave it to his son Richard, "Little R," and told him to ask me to read it at his funeral. Reading that letter, though touching and hopeful, was one of the hardest things I had ever done. In the letter, Big R told Zac that he hoped and prayed that one day he would be able to live his dream of being a police dispatcher. Big R is still loved and greatly missed by our family and I am often reminded of his influence when I see the pictures of the two of them in Zac's room. What a blessing a friend can be!

A friend, a mentor, a buddy! Big R certainly played those roles in the life of Zac Cannady. He gave so much of his own time to visit Zac, take him places, and teach him about law enforcement, giving him the benefit of more than 25 years of personal experience. Big R gave Zac the badge he received when he became a Captain and that badge, along with another one, is mounted in a shadow box and hangs on Zac's bedroom wall. Big R taught Zac a lot about law enforcement, but he taught him something far more important about living a good life; he taught him about being a friend.

For any of us to truly live our dreams, we need others—to teach us, help us, love us, and share the beauty and joy of life with us. Big R did all of that with Zac. I encourage you to bring your dream to life by finding a friend. A friend that can share the ups and downs with you, a friend that will stick closer than a brother or sister, a friend that will be with you always, in good times and bad, a friend who will love you unconditionally. The best way to have a friend is to be one. Show interest in others, love them, spend time with them and maybe, just maybe, no—most probably, you will develop a friendship that will allow you to truly live your dream.

Zac dressed and ready to ride patrol with "Big R"

Zac and "Big R" at Zac's Birthday Party

Chapter 13

Aim True: Don't Be Afraid
To Pull The Trigger

To ACHIEVE YOUR DREAM, YOU need to define the ultimate goal. In life, windows of opportunity often present themselves, but we fail to act, to take advantage of the moment that could make a crucial difference. I had this experience with job opportunities early in my career, feeling a sure call from God to go in a specific direction, but I was too afraid to act on that feeling. Later in life, I learned that if you really want to live your dream, you have to be willing to pull that trigger—to take the necessary actions, to assume the risk, if you want the reward.

I learned this lesson from an experience with Zac when he was about sixteen years old. Zac loved playing video games and one of his favorites was the Play Station game "deer hunter." He loved pulling that gun trigger and trying to shoot the video deer. A friend from church, Gary Nelson, knew Zac loved the deer hunting game and asked whether he would like to try deer hunting for real. As you can imagine, Zac was very excited about the possibility of going deer hunting, but we wondered how we could get the wheelchair into the woods. Gary figured out a way; he would roll Zac onto the back of a small trailer and pull it with his four-wheel ATV.

On a Saturday morning at 4 a.m. we met Gary at his hunting club. What an adventure this day turned out to be. When we met Gary it was still dark, but Zac was wide-awake and ready to go. Gary pulled his trailer level with the back of our van and Zac rolled onto the trailer. Gary secured the wheel chair with tie downs and we headed out to the hunting location. I remember looking down from the back seat of the four-wheeler and realizing we were in a creek, a place named Yellow Creek. Understandably it made me a little nervous to know that Zac was on the trailer behind us—in a creek, in the dark. We arrived safely to the hunting spot, where Gary set us up to look out over a lush green field. As daylight broke, Zac was ready. He was decked out in camouflage clothing, had his gun poised and ready, and really looked the part of a deer hunter.

It was a very cold morning, but we toughed it out for several hours, all to no avail. We didn't see one deer; but Zac was not discouraged. He kept very quiet, an unusual experience for him; he didn't even want to talk to me. I was freezing, but unbelievably Zac said he wasn't cold in the least. When Gary, who had been hunting in another location, came back for us around noon, we packed up and headed home. Despite not even seeing a deer, let along getting a shot at one, Zac was thrilled with this new experience. The important thing wasn't getting a deer, it was that he gave it a try, he did his best, and he had fun.

The next deer season another church friend, Jimmy Segars, offered to take Zac deer hunting at his cousin's farm in New Hope, Alabama. Jimmy assured us the farm was filled with deer and that Zac would at least see one, if not get a chance to shoot at one. Going to the farm was a much easier process since we could hunt in the afternoon; not having to be up at four in the morning certainly made the prospect more attractive.

Zac's friend and fellow deer hunter, Anthony Mosley, loaned him a Remington .243 caliber rifle with a Bushnell 45 scope, which proved to be a great gun for Zac. The rifle had a shortened stock that made it much easier for Zac to hold and see through the scope. Before we went to the hunting location, Zac practiced using the gun to get comfortable with the feel. I purchased a tripod, which we painted with camouflage, and cut a piece of wood for Zac to position the rifle on, making it easy for him to hold the rifle steady while he waited for a deer to show up. Zac once again suited up in his camouflage, ready and excited to try for a deer once more. I prayed and asked God to please let Zac see a deer that day. When we got the hunting club, we unloaded Zac with the wheelchair lift and positioned him in the bed of Jimmy's dark blue Chevy pickup truck, where we proceeded on a very rough ride to the hunting spot. Zac didn't mind the bumpy trip because he was doing something he loved.

I got into the back of the truck with Zac, helped him load the rifle and set up the tripod for him. As I leaned over to place the tripod in front of him, I looked out and sure enough, there stood a deer in the edge of a thicket. The deer was about eighty yards away, standing dead still and staring directly at us. Dead is about to be the key word! I told Zac to be quiet and not move, fully suspecting that the deer would quickly bolt. Once the tripod was set, I handed the loaded rifle to Zac and told him to look through the scope and find the deer, if it was still out there. It only took him a minute or two to locate the deer. I told him it was all his, to just pretend he was on the play station game— get the deer in the cross hairs of the scope, just at the shoulder line of the deer and then pull that trigger.

Zac quickly locked the sight on the deer, pulling the trigger with an air of assurance. The deer jumped straight up, moving about 10 feet, before falling to the ground. I was so excited, that I jumped off the back of the truck and ran to the deer, Jimmy quickly following suit. When we reached the deer, we could see that Zac had made a perfect shot straight thru the shoulder; the deer was already dead. We drug the deer out of the brush and to the truck where Jimmy field dressed him. We could hardly believe it. In the first ten minutes, Zac had achieved the goal, killing a young male deer with antlers beginning to bud. I am not sure who was more excited—Zac, Jimmy, or me.

Zac continued to hunt for several more hours but there were no more deer that day. We loaded up and headed for home, arriving about 6:00 p.m. where Jimmy dressed the deer in our garage. We hung the deer up by his heels from the garage doorframe; cut off the tender loin, which we fried and ate with biscuits and gravy—a Southern favorite. What an amazing experience for Zac, shooting his first deer while perched in his wheel chair on the back of a pick-up truck. The smile on his face was almost as big as the entire deer.

As I reflected on the day, it was hard to imagine how perfectly it all came together; being in that space, that time, at precisely the right moment. The first try with the tripod, the first aim of the day, the first shot of the rifle and voila—Zac gets his deer. Zac prophetically declared, "That deer had a death wish." I was so thankful to God that Zac had this wonderful experience; but I also learned a lesson that day. If you want to live your dream, hit your target, there are some important steps you need to take. First, aim straight; make sure you have your sights set on the target you want to achieve. Second, and even more importantly, have the courage to actually pull the trigger. Life offers many opportunities; opportunities that sometimes present themselves when we are too afraid to respond. When opportunity comes your way, do not be afraid to pull the trigger. You have to take the chance, step out in faith, and respond with boldness. So go ahead, take that job, walk that isle, take that leap of faith. If you want to live your dream, aim true, and don't be afraid to pull the trigger!

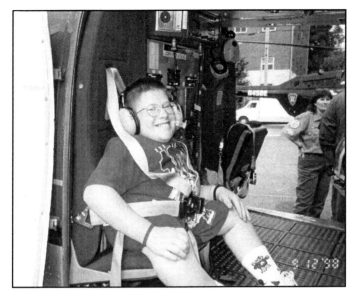

Zac strapped in "Med-flight helicopter" on 911 day

Zac with the deer he shot

Chapter 14

Education: Continue To Learn

IF YOU WANT TO TRULY live your dreams, to fulfill your purpose in life, and enjoy all that the world has to offer, you need to appreciate the value of education. This need not necessarily be education in the formal sense, attending an institution of higher learning, but it does mean taking advantage and learning from the opportunities available to you. It means growing as a person, understanding yourself, and learning practical knowledge, common sense, about the world you live in. It is critical to utilize your education to its fullest advantage. What I'm referring to is much more than reading, writing and arithmetic. ABCs and 123s are important; they are vital to living a successful life, but there are more important aspects to living the dream. I did not fully understand the importance of education until I was suddenly the father of a handicapped son; opportunities easily available to others, would not necessary be something Zac could benefit from.

Shortly after Zac began to crawl, he managed to get to the curtains at the sliding glass door, where he began to pull himself up. It looked as if he was trying to climb up the window using the curtains. Karen, like any good mother normally would, scolded him to stop. Of course, she was worried that he could hurt himself. However, I distinctly remember saying these words to her, "Do not tell him no. He needs to be able to do everything he can possibly do. Do not discourage him by telling him no."

Zac began his public education at West End Elementary school in the kindergarten class of Mrs. Francis Marsh. Sending Zac to public school was a fearful thing for Karen and me because of our concerns about wheelchair access and catherization, among others. Our fears were quickly overcome when the school system made every effort to accommodate Zac's physical needs. But one of the first things he heard, that he didn't hear much of at home, was NO. He had to learn to comply with the teacher's rules.

In kindergarten, a valuable part of his education began to emerge. Zac had to learn to sit still while everyone was taking their nap. But Zac didn't like being still, so he would just unlock the wheelchair brake and slip out the door, going across the hall to visit with kids in another classroom. The teacher, wanting to teach him discipline and the meaning of no, without upsetting him, found a solution. Mrs. Marsh got two broom handles and slid them in the tire spokes so he couldn't roll away. This was the beginning of a real education for Zac. He loved Mrs. Marsh and being in kindergarten, but he also learned the meaning of the word no.

The next year, his first grade teacher was Mrs. Wanda Pollard; she was a great teacher and became a dear friend of our family. In Mrs. Pollard's class Zac learned about having and being a friend when she brought a dog to school to serve as the class pet. Her family raised dogs, so she brought a shiatsu puppy to class named Me Li. Zac and Me Li fell in love with each other. Me Li would ride around the school sitting on the wheelchair footrest, which obviously attracted attention to Zac, but it also made the kids feel comfortable with Zac and his wheelchair. Because of Me Li, and thanks to Mrs. Pollard, Zac made a lot of great friends that year, people who are still friends today. Education is also about learning how to get along with others, being open and accepting, and gaining the acceptance of others. Thank God Zac got such a good start in the early years of his education.

In Middle school there were new challenges when Zac decided to participate in the marching band. He had loved the Aggie Band since he was three years old when I would hold him in my arms at the football games and he would direct the band from the stands, waving his arms in time with the music. Now he wanted to participate. The band directors were great with Zac and helped him choose the xylophone as his instrument. Zac learned to hit the right notes and guide the other band members, developing a knack for teamwork and accomplishing a common goal. The band was a big commitment, with practice every day, but Zac was up for it; he loved music.

I will never forget the first time he "marched" with the band in the homecoming parade. We had to find a way for him to play as he rolled along the street, so my Dad mounted the xylophone to the base of the chair allowing him to easily sit and play. But he couldn't play and roll himself at the same time, so I was the means for movement. I had the great privilege of pushing his wheelchair along the streets of Albertville for several miles on a hot fall day. Zac and I, as part of the junior Aggie band, made the trip through downtown playing the Aggie fight song on the xylophone. What a day to remember.

By the time Zac entered high school, he gave up on the band. He had other things on his mind, like the Police department and eventually becoming a dispatcher there. We dropped him off every day for four years at Albertville High School, a place where he made new friends and overcame other obstacles. The campus consisted of several buildings, some multi-level, so now it wasn't just a matter of getting down the hall to the next class, but from building to building and floor to floor. To be sure he could get around easily and quickly, we got his first electric wheel chair.

One of the funniest things that happened involved the school elevator. I was at home that day when the phone rang, and the school principal, Johnny Ingram, said, "Mr. Cannady, I need to tell you that there is a problem at school." As you can imagine, my heart jumped into my throat and my mind began to race before he had a chance to explain. I was so scared about what might have happened to Zac. We had worried for years about the cars, the steps, and the curbs. Before I almost fainted, Mr. Ingram informed me that Zac was stuck in an elevator in the junior high building. The good news was that he was fine and not alone. A substitute teacher, Mr. Fred Engleman, was stuck in the elevator with him. As you can imagine, the principal was very afraid that we would be upset and even more concerned about Zac and possible trauma.

Karen and I jumped in the van and drove quickly to the school, which was only a few miles away. By the time we arrived, the elevator was open, Zac was free and having a good laugh. He really found this situation hilarious, laughing and joking about it for days. And the best news, at least for Zac, was that he was allowed to get out of school early that day. This too was part of Zac's education; he learned how to handle adversity and still keep a sense of humor.

In 2004 Zac graduated from Albertville High School. It was a great day for the entire family since eighteen years before we could have never imagined that we would see him roll across that stage and pick up his diploma. It was a very special day in our lives and we celebrated with a big party at the family life center of our church. Many friends and family were in attendance and Zac was more than happy to be the center of attention. We all had a great time, but Zac loved every minute of it. Such a milestone may not seem like a big achievement for most children, but for a child that wasn't expected to live a few hours, this was a special moment. Not only was he alive and well, he had graduated from High School!

Education is a vital part of living your dreams; never stop learning. Zac's education certainly did not stop after he finished high school. He continues to learn and grow each and every day. I know for me as well, I desire to learn something new every day of my life. If you want to live your dream, continue to learn.

Chapter 15

Persevere: The Voice On the Radio

IN THE SPRING OF 2007, after three years of hard work, Zac completed another major accomplishment: He graduated from Snead State Junior College in Boaz, Alabama, with an associate's degree in Criminal Justice. It had been difficult and trying at times, but Zac knew he needed a degree to work at the police department. He was so proud of himself; we all were. At the graduation ceremony he was wearing that trademark smile and enjoying every minute of this truly momentous occasion. But as joyous as that day was, he was even more thrilled on his first day as a police dispatcher. At last he was able to wear his Albertville Police shirt and actually get to talk on the police radio.

The Albertville Police Communications Officer, Scott Lacks, developed a schedule where Zac could work six hours per day, five days a week. He worked Monday through Friday from 6 a.m. until

95

noon. Normally dispatch jobs required working swing shifts, sometimes all night long. Since this was obviously more than Zac could handle, Scott worked out this special schedule with the Chief of Police, Benny Womack. Zac worked thirty hours per week and for him, that was a pretty grueling schedule. Getting up and getting ready for work, especially that early in the day, and answering 911 calls created more than a little bit of stress.

In the fall of 2007, Zac finally had the job he had wanted since he was seven years old. Those first few days, after I dropped him off at work, I would come home, turn on the police scanner and listen to his voice on the radio. For almost fifteen years he had dreamed of this, and now he was doing it every day. My heart was filled with pride.

To achieve his dream, we had to overcome some significant challenges. The Department of Rehabilitation for the State of Alabama provided assistance to make the workspace accessible for Zac. Janice Creel helped developed the necessary changes and the Rehab program modified the space to accommodate Zac. Zac also had to complete special training for the National Crime Institute Computer (NCIC) and communications training. Zac had to be at work at 6 a.m., so that meant getting up at 4:30 a.m. every weekday; this was a real chore for all of us. We had to get to bed early to make that four thirty alarm and do everything necessary for him to be at work on time. Before, Zac never wanted to get up early, but going to work at the police station was motivation enough.

Everyone at the police department seemed to enjoy working with Zac. A lot of them already knew Zac and since he never meets a stranger he soon knew all of the policemen. Scott Lacks, Zac's boss, loved him and was always bragging on the good job he was doing. Zac developed a great working relationship with Matthew Shipp, who also worked in the dispatch room and the two of them became very good friends. In June of 2008, the local newspaper featured an article about Zac and his work at the police department, highlighting the fact that he was "living his dream". A national magazine picked up the story on the wire and called to ask if they could also publish a story about Zac. The October 2008 edition of *The Journal of Emergency Dispatch* included an article about Zac's inspirational work, complete with a color photograph of him sitting at the dispatch console. The article entitled "Living the Dream," shared the story of Zac's dream of being a dispatcher since he was in the second grade. Seeing Zac featured in a national publication was another occasion that filled me with great pride and thankfulness.

At the end of 2008, Zac was awarded the State of Alabama Handicapped Employee of the Year award in a ceremony at the Public Library in Albertville. Several State Employment officials were there to make the award, along with the Albertville Police Chief, Benny Womack, and Communications

Officer, Scott Lacks. Zac also managed to make the 6 p.m. evening news on one of the Huntsville, Alabama channels. It was another memorable day for us to celebrate Zac accomplishments.

At last Zac was enjoying his dream job, the thing he had most wanted to do in life—being a police dispatcher. The lesson I learned from this achievement was one of perseverance. For more than fifteen years he had hoped for, worked towards, and prepared well for this goal. Now, it was truly a dream come true for Zac. If you want to live your dream, one thing you will need plenty of is perseverance! Work hard, jump through the hoops, and keep a firm belief that you can make it happen. Zac hoped and prayed, he persevered until he reached that pinnacle, he became the police dispatcher he had always wanted to be. You see, sometimes dreams really do come true.

Chapter 16

Prayer: It Keeps Your Dream Alive

As 2009 ROLLED AROUND, ZAC was growing more and more tired with each passing day. When I reread the article in the local paper, I noticed Zac's response to the question about the hardest part of the job—"I just get really tired." The work schedule was tiring for his small frame and getting up so early was really wearing him down. He went through a difficult period and made the decision to stop working. There were a lot of physical problems that left him without sufficient energy to make it through the workday. Little did we know that his was a downward trend that would result in Zac getting very sick in 2010. As the year wore on, he was slowing down, spending more time in his room. We had hoped he might be able to return to work, but he said no, that it was too stressful for him. The very thing he had loved almost as much as life itself seemed to be taking a toll on him. As summer came, he grew even quieter and almost never wanted to go anywhere. When we built our house in 2004, we installed a swimming pool with a lift for Zac. Ever since he was a small child, he loved swimming; he was great in the water, amazing everyone with his ability swim despite his paralysis. But now he refused to get into the swimming pool.

As the summer wore on his tiredness only increased and by the first of August he struggled to make it through the day. On Sunday, August 8th we attended a church picnic in Guntersville, where Zac sat alone with his police scanner for most of the event. In the Retreat Center kitchen, I remember him sitting at the end of the table occasionally talking with a friend from church, Lisa Thomas. The next day we were planning to watch the Atlanta Braves baseball game in the afternoon. He loves the Braves and that day a new rookie pitcher, Mike Minor, was to take the mound for his first big league start. Zac was ready to check him out but he felt so bad that he asked me to get him out of his wheelchair so he could sit on the sofa. This was very unusual, Zac never got out of his chair during the daytime. As the game began, I noticed his color was bad and he felt cold and clammy. I asked him if we should go to the hospital to check things out, but he wasn't sure he wanted to go. When I suggested we call the ambulance he gave in; seems that he knew the ambulance drivers on call that night and Zac was up for a ride with them.

I called the city dispatch and explained Zac's symptoms and within minutes Rescue 1, the Albertville ambulance, arrived with two of Zac's buddies. They checked him out and we decided to go to the local hospital for further analysis. We arrived at the hospital around 7 p.m. and went into the emergency room where the medical personnel began a series of tests. They ordered blood and urine cultures, checked his vitals —his blood pressure was low, but his heart rate was high, 145 beats per minute. After several hours of waiting, it was determined he had a urinary tract infection and the ER doctor said he needed to stay overnight and get intravenous antibiotics for the infection. Since the hospital room was so small, Karen stayed with Zac and I came home.

The next morning when I arrived at the hospital, Zac was not feeling much better. They ordered more tests and sent him for a scan. When he came back to his room he was feeling even worse and seemed upset. Over the next few hours, he got progressively worse; eventually he was not alert and could not even talk to us. I decided we needed to transfer him to Children's Hospital where his doctors had taken care of him for twenty-five years. I talked with Dr. David Joseph, who has been Zac's life-long urologist, and he agreed to admit him to Children's if the local hospital completed transfer orders. After much discussion and help from my friend James Minor, who was Zac's nurse that day, the orders were signed and the ambulance transported Zac to Birmingham. As he left for the trip, Zac was incoherent and we would later learn that his CO2 was extremely high, causing disorientation. I remember when they loaded him into the ambulance and closed the door, I began to cry; he was so sick, I wasn't sure he would make it to Birmingham alive.

Karen had already left for Birmingham to be there when the ambulance arrived. I left in our van, alone. Zac was supposed to go directly to the special care unit but during the trip, I received a call telling me to come directly to the emergency room at Children's. When I arrived at the ER, I was rushed to the trauma room where Karen was waiting with Dr. Joseph. The medical personnel were intubating Zac and using a bag to help him breathe. The atmosphere in the room was frantic and there were sixteen people working on Zac, doing their best to keep him alive. The ER Doctor, the Intensive Care Unit (ICU) Doctor, and Dr. Joseph had a discussion about whether to transfer Zac to the University of Alabama hospital just blocks away or whether to admit him to Children's. He was twenty-four years old, hardly a child; but it was decided they could better care for him at Children's. The ICU Doctor said he would develop a treatment plan and asked that we give him some time to work with Zac. We were told to wait upstairs in the Pediatric Intensive Care Unit (PICU) waiting area; the Doctor would meet with us there once he had developed his "game plan."

The wait seemed like an eternity, though in reality, it was only about two hours. At 9 p.m. the Doctor took us into a small family consulting room and shared his findings and plans. He said, "Your son is very sick, we have placed him in an induced coma. He is septic, and I would say that he has a seventy five percent chance of not making it through the night." He also informed us that the next twelve hours were the most critical and then the next twenty-four vital. If Zac could make it for twelve hours his odds of pulling through would greatly increase. He had a very serious infection, which had moved into his blood stream and was attacking his body. They weren't sure of the type of infection or what antibiotic it might respond to, so they were administering a cocktail of antibiotics, hoping to stop it quickly. I will never forget the Doctor saying, "We want to give Zac the very best chance at surviving this." That was encouraging; encouraging words make a difference in our lives, especially when you are facing such a grim situation. At least now we knew what was happening with Zac and felt sure he was in the best possible care. That too was encouraging.

We did the only thing we knew to do at that moment—we prayed, earnestly, for God to help Zac pull though. We prayed, as if it was a matter of life and death, in fact, it truly was. Often in our lives, we pray without much enthusiasm, but in times of crisis we pray as if nothing else matters, because it doesn't. But, how unfortunate that it takes a crisis for us to get serious with our prayers. Our family was with us, and soon friends from church began to arrive; the prayer meeting began.

We all huddled in a corner of the PICU waiting room on the third floor at Children's Hospital and called on the Lord, to be with and intervene on Zac's behalf, to make him well again.

I had always said that Zac was one of the most prayed for kids I had ever seen. Even before his birth, and throughout his life, people in our state and beyond had prayed for him. Now, at this moment, again in Children's Hospital and faced with life and death, all we seemed able to do was PRAY! Pray and ask God for Zac to make it thru the night, to get to 9 a.m. in the morning and then we could go from there.

We all face difficulties and challenges in life. Sometimes it feels like morning is never going to come. Those can be the best times to truly, sincerely, call on the name of the Lord. In the Bible, God told Jeremiah to call unto me and I will answer you and show you great and mighty things you do not know. That night we needed great and mighty things to happen, so we called on God for answers to our prayers. The Bible certainly contains some great promises and this one to Jeremiah helped us make it thru that night.

When life bears down, and hope seems grim, when doctors may not have all the answers, call on HIM—God the Father, Jesus the Son and The Holy Spirit—our comforter and guide. The power of faith and prayer are powerful tools for overcoming crisis and for fulfilling your dreams.

Chapter 17

Hope: Always Hope of Being "Better Than Ever"

Zac did indeed pull through those next twelve hours. At 9 a.m. Wednesday morning there was a sigh of relief, though we weren't out of the woods yet, at least he had made it thought that critical twelve-hour period. For the next twenty-four hours we visited with him, prayed for him and asked all of our friends and family to pray for Zac. When we went in to see him first thing that morning, he was heavily sedated and I counted the IV lines, nine. Zac was hooked to a ventilator that was breathing for him. I was amazed at all the interventions the doctors were making with him. They were giving him several types of antibiotics, hoping that one of them would be the right one to ward off the infection that was attacking his body. But it could take several days before we knew for sure if any of them were succeeding.

We learned that morning how Zac struggled during the night, his heart rate getting so low he required chest compressions. He continued to struggle, but he succeeded in making that critical hurdle, he made it through that twenty-four hour period. We were hopeful, prayerful that he would turn the corner, even as he remained in a medically induced coma, breathing only with the aid of the ventilator. Prayers, cards, food, well wishes were pouring in from around the world; they came through Facebook, emails, and in person.

After several days, the doctors decided to bring Zac, at least partially, out of the coma. He was still on the ventilator and running a fever but the doctors felt it was time to see how he would respond. I was in the ICU visiting him when he opened his eyes enough to see me. I told him it was Friday night at 12:30 a.m. and he raised his eyebrows as if say, "What?" He obviously could not believe that he had lost three days. The doctors finally determined he had several types of infection, the worst of which was pseudomonas, classified as a super bug. Now that the doctors knew the types of infections they were dealing with, they were able to determine the appropriate medications and cut back on some of the IVs.

Prayers continued to pour in for Zac over that weekend. The doctors placed a main IV line in Zac's groin to inject all the meds he needed. Over the weekend, he made progress and was even weaned from the ventilator on Sunday afternoon. Once weaned, they were able to move him out of the PICU to the Special Care Unit. As you can imagine, we were very excited, things were looking up for Zac. Zac was thrilled to be in the SCU, since his best friend Shannon Sharit was the charge nurse in this unit and she would take extra special care of him. Over the weekend, there were lots of visitors to lift our spirits and show their support. On Sunday night, Maggee Oliver, a church member and friend of Zac's, stayed all night with him in the Special Care Unit. Zac loved this because he had been a friend with Maggee for many years. We knew her family because they went to church with Karen's parents. Maggee was now a student at the Samford University pharmacy school in Birmingham and it was wonderful to have her so close by and able to visit with Zac.

Unfortunately, on Monday, August 16, Zac wasn't feeling well and only got worse as the day wore on. Finally, I called for the Doctor to find out what was happening. He was a young Urology intern, working with Dr Joseph, and he did not seem to understand what we were telling him. Zac was responding, or failing to respond, exactly as he had at Medical Center North when we discovered his CO_2 was too high. When I asked the Doctor to check the CO_2 level he said it would take several hours to get the results. I informed him that the PICU, just around the corner, could get the reading in a matter of minutes. They drew the blood for the test and took it to the PICU.

In the meantime, Zac was fading in and out; it was as if he were just going away, falling into a deep sleep. Karen was with him talking to and encouraging him to stay with her. In just a few minutes, the nurse ran into the room and handed the doctor the CO2 report, it was 103. The normal rate is below thirty. The medical staff went into immediate action, hurrying Zac back to ICU and placing him back on the ventilator. Suddenly, our hopes were dashed and we found ourselves back in a very difficult place.

Karen and I held each other in the hallway and cried as we watched Zac whisked down the hall and back to the PICU. We were standing in almost the very spot we stood and held each other 24 years ago. Oh my; what a day this had turned into. The whole family was stunned and saddened as we lingered in the hallway for a report of what was happening. It was my sister's birthday; and as she said, it was the worst birthday ever.

The ICU doctor informed us that Zac was in respiratory failure; his lungs were not processing the oxygen and disposing of the CO2 properly. The only thing we could do at this point was to place him back on the ventilator, try to build up his strength, and pray that his lungs would get better. So that is what we did, and we prayed even more than before. I asked everyone to pray that Zac would be "Better than ever!"

We were all exhausted, having had little sleep for almost a week. None of us wanted to leave and someone, usually several of us, were in the waiting room or at Zac's bedside at all times. On Tuesday afternoon I was on the verge of collapse and after much insistence from family, I went for a nap at the Children's Harbor. This is a facility attached to the hospital where parents and siblings of children in the hospital can get some rest, shower, have snacks, and even play games. They have sleep rooms with a futon bed, a chair, and a small lamp. I signed in and went to my room. It was comforting to have a place to lie down in the dark and yet, not be far from Zac and the family.

Once asleep, I had an amazing and enlightening dream. In my dream, Zac and I were standing somewhere I had never seen before; it was just outside the gates of heaven. Only the two of us were there, he was in his wheel chair and I was standing beside him. I was actually between him and the gates. We were amazed at what we saw; there were two very large arched gates that met in the middle. To the left side of the middle of the gates was a small door that opened. The door was only large enough for one person to pass through at a time. As the door opened a strong, bright light flooded out through the doorway, a light so strong that you were almost blinded until your eyes adjusted. As soon as my eyes were able to focus, I looked through the door and saw a long street extending upward to the top of a hill. There was a large building at the top of the hill, which was the origin of the light. As we moved closer to the door, I realized that Zac could go in. I moved aside and let him pass by me, telling him to go in if he felt God was leading him to. He looked in, paused, and looked back at me. I encouraged him with all my strength to go through the door. So he rolled his wheelchair to the open door and passed through. As he entered the door, his wheelchair disappeared, his feet hit the ground and he began to walk slowly, never looking back. I woke myself up screaming, "Run Zac run!"

What a dream that was, it felt so very real. My heart was pounding and I was crying, tears of joy for Zac. I felt that dream was directing me to tell Zac it was ok for him to leave us, that our family be fine. I went to his bedside in ICU, where he was still on the ventilator, lots of tubes attached to his body. I leaned over and whispered into his ear, "If God wants you to go home with him, go. It will all be fine for us. We love you but if He calls, you GO!" That was one of the hardest things I had ever said, and how strange to be back exactly where we had been twenty-four years before, once again facing life or death. But this time was different. This time we had twenty-four years of living and memories, happy times we had shared, a special love that had grown over the years. It was much harder now, because there was so much more to miss. But at least we could be thankful for the years we'd been given; no doubt though there would be grief over how much we would lose.

Fortunately, we weren't going to lose him yet. The next day he turned a corner and began to improve.

I just kept repeating, over and over, that we wanted Zac to be "better than ever." People near and far were praying for just that, that he would in fact be "better than ever." Over the next few days he progressed enough to begin weaning him off of the ventilator. This process was very scary to him, as he knew that vent meant life or death. We were careful to explain exactly what was happening and discuss the options with him. During this time, he especially wanted his mother and sister with him as much as possible. We used every trick we could find to make him comfortable. My sister, Teresa, bought a CD player and headphones so he could listen to the Kingdom Heirs, one of his favorite gospel groups. Listening to this beloved gospel music provided a source of comfort and peace. Zac had loved music since he began singing at three years old and at this critical moment it played a special role in his life. Not only did it bring him a sense of peace, but it also drowned out the many noises, especially the crying babies, in the ICU.

On August 20th, they began to wean him off of the ventilator, allowing him more time breathing on his own. Over the course of several hours, they monitored him closely to see how he would respond without the ventilator. Things went well. Finally, the plan was to fully remove the ventilator. Karen and I had already discussed what to do if he experienced the same problem and wasn't able to breathe on his own. It was a hard discussion, but we were in agreement. Once the ventilator was removed, he was quickly placed on a Bi-lateral

Positive Air, or Bi-Pap machine, which has a mask for breathing assistance. The mask was blowing a combination of air and oxygen into his lungs. After twenty-four hours on the Bi-Pap, they began to wean him off so he could try to breathe on his own. At first he was allowed to go without the Bi-Pap for an hour and then his oxygen and carbon dioxide levels were checked. The time between the Bi-Pap and breathing on his own was increased and after a few days he could be moved to a private room. A few days later, the doctors began discussing his release from the hospital. Just the thought of being home was so wonderful. Our hopes were revived that he would soon be back in his bedroom, decorated with University of Alabama football memorabilia.

While Zac was in the hospital people kept giving me money and I was wondering why. I had accumulated almost $2,000, which was now in my wallet. The day before we were released, a sleep study was performed to determine whether Zac needed breathing support at night. Zac was in a sleep lab all night, starting out without any breathing support, which created a lot of anxiety for all of us, especially Zac. Within the first hour his stats were already dropping so low that he was placed on the bi-pap. The following morning we returned to his room on the pulmonary floor, where the doctors began preparing him to go home. The doctors told us, based on the study, that Zac had to have a bi-pap machine for sleeping; otherwise he would have the same problem with carbon dioxide. Arrangements were made to obtain the equipment and have it delivered to our house; we would go home the following morning.

Unexpectedly, later in the day we were told that our insurance provider would not cover the costs of a bi-pap machine at home. We were very upset and worried by this news; how could he go home without the machine? I asked the hospital staff how much the machine would cost and was told a used one similar to the hospital version could run as much as $5,000. I was very distraught; it just didn't seem possible to make this happen. But then I asked for the telephone number of the medial supply company they recommended. When I spoke with the salesperson he told me they had a machine in stock, which they could program to Zac's specification. The moment of truth came when I asked for the price. He checked and replied, "It is $1,800 dollars for the machine we have in stock, brand new." I immediately opened my wallet and counted the cash people had been giving me; there was $1,800. Praise the Lord, He knew what we needed before the need even arose. I asked the salesman to deliver the bi-pap to our house the next afternoon, glad that we would be home to receive it. God is Good!

Zac not only came home the next day, but he did it in style. He called his friends at the Albertville Fire department and arrangements were made for him to be picked up in the city ambulance by two of his buddies. Richard Soper, "Little Sop" as Zac called him, would ride in the back of the ambulance to take care of Zac. We were so thankful to be brining Zac back home. Thanks to the prayers of many, many, people, and to God's grace, Zac came home from the hospital on August 26th, not totally well, but well enough to sleep in his own bed. Thank the Lord, and thanks to all of those who prayed and gave money for the bi-pap machine.

There can be no doubt that when living our dreams, we will be faced with difficulties and struggles that can only be overcome with prayer and a lot of love from people around us, sometimes even people we don't know. But with that love and support, we can always live with hope. Hope that helps make those dreams a reality. Thanks to a lot of love and care, Zac was at that moment "better than ever!"

Chapter 18

Be Aware: Opportunities Are Around You

GOD HAS BLESSED ALL OF us with special gifts, talents we possess and things we love to do. When we use these gifts, not only are our lives enriched, but they also bring a blessing to others around us. None of us can live our dream in a vacuum. What you do impacts others, hopefully in a positive way. Living our dreams brings a new source of strength, an energy inside of us that can't be contained. We saw this vividly demonstrated in Zac's love for singing and his love for dispatching. The two may not seem to have a lot in common, other than using your voice, but they have brought him great joy. When Zac sings, he feels the presence of God and is empowered by the Spirit of God within him. When you see him sing you will see the energy, feel it, even catch it for yourself. Ever since his first public singing appearance at the Bible School commencement, Zac has found joy in singing and in sharing his special gift with others.

Zac's favorite lists of songs were developed from the Red Back Church Hymnal used at Antioch Baptist Church where his grandparents attended church. He developed a great love for the traditional church hymns such as "I'll Fly Away," "Amazing Grace," and others. When he attended services at Antioch, they would often invite him to lead a song for the congregation. Well, you can imagine how much he loved having that opportunity; and I think the congregation enjoyed listening to him just as much. When he could not go to a service, someone would bring him a tape of the service so he could listen and learn the songs. He began to memorize the page numbers for every song. If you said the title of a song, he could quickly tell you the page where it was located.

Zac furthered his love of gospel music by watching videos of Bill Gaither. He wanted every one of them and we often bought him videotapes as gifts for his birthday or Christmas. In addition to Bill Gaither, he also developed an interest in the Happy Goodman Family, the Speer family, and JD Sumner and the Stamps Quartet. He loved those traditional gospel singers, but eventually he also expanded his interest to some of the more contemporary gospel singers such as Ivan Parker. Zac first met Ivan Parker when he was still a young fellow and Ivan's group, the Gold City Quartet, sang at the Bevill Center in Boaz. Zac had a front row seat and met all the members of the group, who gave him an autographed t-shirt.

We live less than five hours drive from the Smoky Mountains in Tennessee and often vacation there, usually staying in either Pigeon Forge or Gatlinburg. We all love Dollywood theme park, where we met a gospel group named the Kingdom Heirs. They sing in the park almost every day and when Zac discovered them, he wanted to attend every show. Some days he would go to four of their shows; he was in love with their music. But beyond the music, he met and made friends with members of the group. After getting to know them fairly well, we decided to ask them to help with a fundraiser for our friend Steve Redmond, who was injured an automobile accident in 2002 while on a church mission trip. Steve was left paralyzed from the neck down from the accident.

In February 2005, we hosted the Kingdom Heirs in the first of several fundraising concerts. At one of the concerts, Zac opened the program by singing "Beulah Land" to an audience of about than 500 people. What a great experience for Zac to share his voice with all these people, especially for such a great cause. These concerts allowed Zac to build his friendship with the members of the group including their tenor at that time, Billy Hodges. Billy had been a fireman before joining the group, so the two of them had an immediate connection. Billy gave Zac his fireman's badge, which is framed, along with Big R's Captain badge, in the shadow box in Zac's room.

One night, several years ago, we were eating dinner at Red Lobster in Gadsden, Alabama when we saw Howard and Vestel Goodman, of the Happy Goodman family. Zac, never afraid to meet new people, rolled his wheel chair right up to their table and started a conversation. He said, "Hey there, you are Vestal Goodman aren't you?" She smiled and said, "Yeah, I certainly am young man." Zac told them how he loved to sing and how much he loved their group. They had a nice talk and Vestel seemed to really love Zac.

On another occasion, Zac was invited to open an Ivan Parker concert in Albertville. When we arrived, we met Ivan backstage and he remembered meeting Zac when he was with the Gold City Quartet. Zac opened the program with one of his favorite songs, "Beulah Land." As Zac was singing, Ivan was so moved that he asked me whether he could join Zac onstage and finish the song. Ivan took his stool out, sat down beside Zac, placed his hand on Zac's shoulder and they performed the second verse as a duet. What a great experience for Zac, fueling his fire to find more opportunities to sing and share his gift.

We were very worried about whether Zac's singing ability would be affected by his illness and the time spent on the ventilator in August 2010. But our fears were allayed when, in the spring of 2011, we met a new group, named Rhyme and Reason. The group performed a revival at our church in March 20ll and Zac hit it off with their leader and evangelist, Wayne Chasteen. They loved gospel music and Wayne grew very fond of Zac. After the revival was over, Wayne invited us to visit him in Olgethrope, Georgia—near Chattanooga, Tennessee—on our next trip to the Smoky Mountains.

In June, on our way home from a short trip to the Great Smoky Mountains, we stopped and had lunch with Wayne Chasteen and Mary McKinley. Mary works with Rhyme and Reason as their piano player. Wayne has a recording studio in the back of his office, and since we had never seen one we asked for a tour. We were inspired to have Zac record a CD of his favorite old gospel hymns and asked if that would be possible. Wayne replied, "For Zac, it will be free of charge, if we can arrange it in the next few weeks when I'm not traveling."

We set a date and time for the recording and Zac asked his second cousin, Vanessa Kirby to accompany him on the piano. Vanessa had played the piano years before when Zac sang at Antioch church. Zac developed a list of songs he wanted to sing and gave them to Vanessa. We went to the studio in Oglethorpe, where Wayne set everything up, first recording the music tracks, and experimenting with the vocals, to determine the right mix. Vanessa played for several hours as they recorded songs like *What a Day That Will Be, Amazing Grace, O Come Angel Band*, among others. It took almost the entire day to finish but Zac was filled with energy and patience to make it happen. Once they finished the music tracks, Wayne said he would lay the tracks so Zac could return and complete the vocals.

The following week Zac, Karen, and I returned to the studio where Zac recorded the final vocals. It was truly amazing to see Zac sing; he seemed to get stronger the more he sang. It's interesting that living your dream strengthens you rather than exhausting you. There is an energy that comes from God, which builds us up as we work to fulfill our dreams. I certainly saw that effect with Zac. He finished the CD and entitled it *This is My Story, This is My Song*. The first track on the CD was a recording of Zac when he was only three years old. His grandfather, Jerry Beam, had recorded Zac on a cassette tape and Wayne was able to include the recording as the introduction to the CD. The song is *Blessed Assurance*, written by a blind woman named Fannie Crosby. The chorus of the song says, "This is my story this is my song, praising my Savior all the day long" and thus the name of Zac's first CD.

Living your dream is a state of mind. You need to feel that you are making a difference, not only for yourself, but also in the lives of others. Zac's music, while bringing a lot of joy to him, has certainly made a lot of difference in the lives of others. As you live your dream, know that your strength can be renewed as you respond to opportunities around you that allow you to make a difference in the world.

Chapter 19

How Zac Helped Me;
"Live My Dream"!

THERE IS ANOTHER IMPORTANT RESULT of Zac living his dream—the effect he has had on me. Zac's influence led me to an entirely new avenue in my life. Since the age of eighteen I had felt a calling, but refused to act on it. I had kept this dream in the back of my mind and the midst of my heart. Although this urging had been present in my life for almost fifteen years, I never found the fortitude to act on it. In fact, I usually tried to push it away and forget it and while I could sometimes keep it at bay, it was still buried beneath the surface, and always found a way to resurface. Every time I prayed for guidance, I heard the same answer, "You know what I want." God was responding to me but I wasn't responding to him. I truly believed that God had created me to be a spokesman for Him, a communicator of His truth, a teacher of

His Word. But I never felt like I was good enough. I never thought anyone would listen to me. So, for many years I struggled with the issue of living the dream that God has placed in my heart. Because of my lack of confidence, I refused to reveal this dream to anyone else.

Today, I wonder how many people have been in that same situation. Knowing that God has placed a dream in their heart, a purpose for their life, but unable to respond to that wonderful opportunity. For whatever reason, many people are afraid to step out in pursuit of that dream. Perhaps because of fear of failure, fear of what others may say, fear of making a dramatic change in their lives. I know those feelings were overpowering my will to follow the dream.

I observed Zac and was inspired by how he was able to respond to the opportunities and the challenges he faced. He was never afraid to be in the public eye, to step out in front of people and sing. He had no fear of doing what he enjoyed and what he believed in. He pursued the police dispatcher job, even when it seemed hopeless; he never gave up. Zac put his passion first and learned to live a life he enjoyed, despite significant obstacles that would've derailed other people. Yes, his start was difficult, more than difficult, but he knew it wasn't about the start, but rather the finish that matters.

I was sure that others would be a much better, more professional, speaker; a better preacher than I could ever hope to be. But I saw Zac not let what his sister could do keep him from doing what only he could do. That truth began to inspire the dream in my heart. In September 1993, when Zac was saved I had the joy of stepping into the baptistery and holding him for our Pastor, Jack Redfearn, to baptize him. I was an eyewitness to the awesome things God was doing around me, but somehow I still was on the outside looking in.

Later that year, I finally surrendered my life to the pursuit of my dream as a communicator of truth and teacher of God's Word. I preached for the first time at Solitude Baptist in Albertville, on November 21, 1993. Zac's lack of fear in almost any situation washed away my nervousness and afforded me the confidence to step forward in faith and speak for the Lord. Seeing Zac overcome all the odds and keep on moving forward gave me the courage I needed to stand up for God. So I stood up and spoke about Peter following Jesus at a distance, sharing the similarities with my own life, explaining how I had followed Him at a distance for the past fifteen years. But today I proclaimed, "My life will change." It was an awesome day as I took that first step towards truly living my dream.

Initially, I only preached as opportunities arose at various churches, but this gave the entire family a great opportunity to go to new places and meet new people. Often Karen and Zac could sing before I did the most awesome thing in the world, communicate God's truth. With each opportunity,

I felt better equipped to do what God had called me to do. My faith deepened and I truly "set my heart" towards the goals of full time Christian service within five years. I completed theology classes at Luther Rice Seminary in Atlanta, while I continued to work my accounting job at Progress Rail Services in Boaz.

In the spring of 1998, our Pastor, Brother Jack Redfearn, was called to the West Hartselle Baptist Church in Hartselle, Alabama. The church asked me to serve as interim pastor while they searched for a replacement. I knew with all my heart God wanted me there; but I could not say that to anyone. So I performed the job they had asked of me, preaching on Sunday mornings, Sunday nights, and Wednesday nights. My first message, as interim pastor, was from Joshua, Chapter six, about the walls of Jericho and how it took faith for those walls to fall. Likewise, it takes faith for us to see our dreams come true. Later that spring the search committee asked if I would consider leaving my position as an Corporate Accountant with Progress Rail to be the full time pastor of Solitude. How amazing! It was four and one half years since the time I set my heart to be able to be in full time ministry. It is amazing how God works when we allow him to.

In June 1998 at age thirty-eight, I accepted the call as the full time Pastor of Solitude Baptist Church. It has been one of the greatest blessings of my life to live out a dream that was placed in my heart when I was eighteen years old. However, I know that I was only able to live this dream due to the leadership of God's Spirit in my heart and because of the many lessons I learned from Zac. Like I said in the beginning, Zac is a pretty good teacher, a teacher of life, of how to not just survive, but to overcome and move past the obstacles that keep you from living your dream.

I know God has placed a dream in all of us that are named among His children. Because of these lessons—it is not how you start, but how you finish that counts; don't give up too quickly; find the silver lining in every cloud—I am still living my dream today, thirteen years and counting as Pastor of Solitude Baptist Church. I still strive to reach my full potential, while wearing my passion, to aim true and not being afraid to pull the trigger. I pray that everyone who reads these words will realize that God has in fact placed a dream in your heart, a special dream, a dream meant only for you.

Recently, God placed another dream in my heart. A dream to write words that will inspire others, motivating them to achieve their highest goals and to truly live their dreams. Know that as you read these words you are helping me to continue to live my dream. But, I hope that you'll do more than just read the words of this short simple little book. I hope you will put these simple principles to work and enjoy that wonderful experience that I am having now—learning, loving, and living My Dream.

Some of you may say that it can't happen for you, that only a few special people get to realize their dreams. Well I know at least two people that have—Zachary Andrew Cannady and me. I also know that you can too. My wish for you is that you find and fulfill your God-given dream so that you can say, as Zac has, "I'm Living My Dream!"

Conclusion

We all face challenges, difficulties, and handicaps in life. However, we can overcome. I especially want each and every parent of a handicapped child to realize, that your son or daughter may be the greatest blessing you will ever know. When Zac was born, it was a painful time filled with doubt and fear about what the future would hold. These past twenty-five years have brought us much joy and many tears. Thankfully, God showed me that our greatest fears could turn into our greatest blessings. For me that has certainly been true. Zac has been and still is, a source of GREAT inspiration, a joy to be with daily, and a continuous lesson of how to live a blessed life, walking with God and depending on him to meet our daily needs.

Zac is still living out his God-given dream. Though he currently isn't working at the police department, he visits there often and talks with many of the officers on a regular basis. He continues to develop new friendships and to collect Police and Fire uniform patches—he has more than 1000 of them and collects more daily. He also continues to pursue his passion for gospel music. Zac has performed at several churches recently, sharing his special brand of gospel music. It is only through God's strength and power that Zac has the energy to sing. Also in December 2011 Zac escorted his "baby sister," Cassie Jo, down the aisle and presented her hand in marriage. What a joy that was to see Zac sharing in this special moment in Cassie's life. I pray daily that Zac will continue to be "Better Than Ever" and continue to fulfill the dreams of his heart. May you be blessed as you pursue your dream as well.

Zac chopped down that cherry tree "all by himself"

Zac marching in parade with middle school Aggie Band

Zac in the "Little Red Car Water Bed"

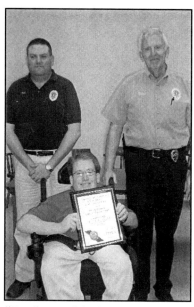

Zac receiving "Employee of the Year Award" in 2008 with Chief
Benny Womack and Communications Officer Scott Lacks

Zac and Ivan Parker after they sang "The duet"

Zac with Cassie after he escorted her down the aisle

Zac's Senior Portrait 2004 - Albertville High School

Zac at the Dispatch Console

CPSIA information can be obtained at www.ICGtesting.com
Printed in the USA
LVOW090056010512

279549LV00001B/2/P